The World of the Arts

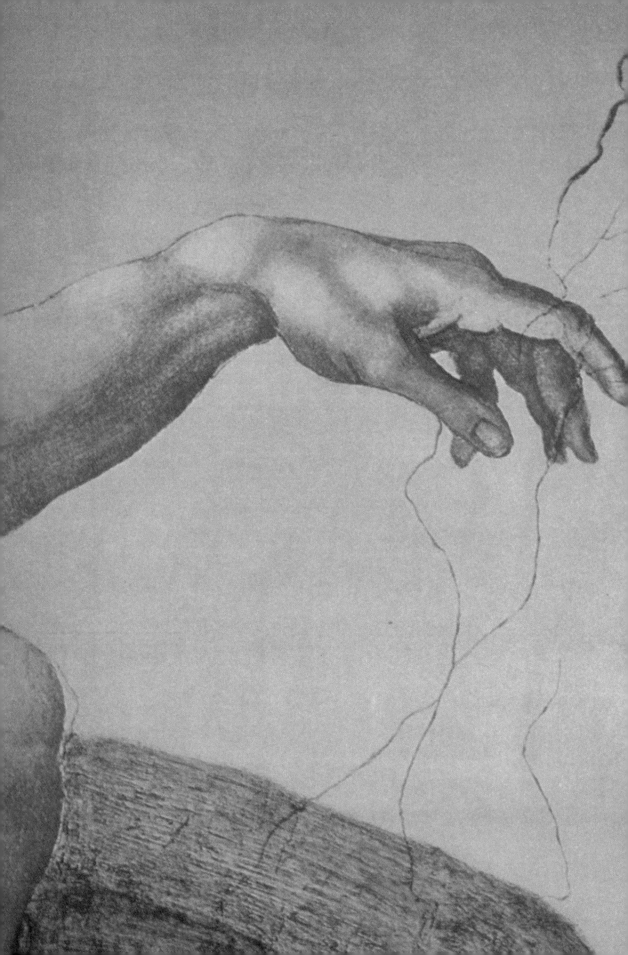

The World of the Arts

by
William Reed

STANDARD EDUCATIONAL CORPORATION   *Chicago 2009*

Library of Congress-in-Publication Data

Reed, William
    The world of the arts / by William Reed
        p. cm
    Summary: Explores various aspects of art, music,
    and drama and their relationship to everyday life.
    ISBN O-87392-307-3
    1. Arts-Juvenille literature. [I. Arts] I. Title.
    NX633.R44 1995
    700' .1-dc20   95-19642
                                                  CIP
                                                  AC

**The huge red stabile named "Flamingo"
by Alexander Calder provides an eye-
catching focal point in Federal Center
Plaza in Los Angeles.**

Previous page: **Detail of the *Creation of
Man*, part of the great Sistine chapel
ceiling fresco painting by Michelangelo.**

AA - 3

Contents

Introduction

You are about to begin a voyage of discovery to a world of wonder and surprise. It is a world that is as old as recorded history and as young as tomorrow. You will not find this world on any map. It has no boundaries, north or south, east or west, yet people of all countries have journeyed there.

In this world there are wonderful things to see— paintings that glow with color, strange masks from far-off lands, and buildings of ageless splendor.

There are wonderful things to hear. Troubadour songs and symphonies fill the air with the sounds of music. There are plays and actors of many kinds. Shadows talk and puppets dance for our pleasure.

Rembrandt and Michelangelo belong to this world. Beethoven and Shakespeare are part of it. An unknown potter in ancient Greece, the people who design houses and bridges, and perhaps you, yourself, belong to it, too.

The world we will explore is the world of the arts, and there are many kinds of arts and many kinds of artists. They work in many different ways, using words to tell a story, or colors to paint a picture, or sounds to make music. Some artists like to depict the everyday world around them, but others go wherever their imagination takes them. In this book you can travel with artists on their journeys of the imagination.

But artists need more than imagination. They have to work hard to put their ideas into a form we can all enjoy. This book takes you into the painter's studio, behind the scenes at the movies, and to many other exciting places to show you the tools and techniques that artists use. We hope that it will help you to understand and love their work.

Still-life with Copper Tankard by the American artist William Harnett (1848-92).

The Visual Arts

Painting and Drawing

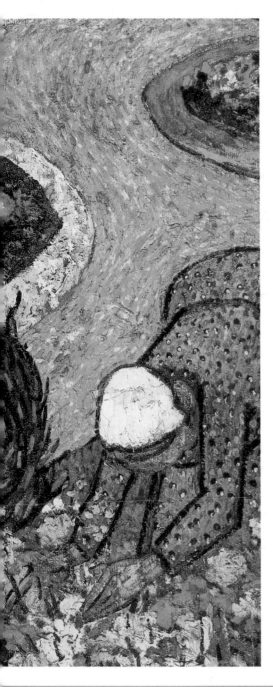

Artists often make many drawings as preparation for their paintings. Sometimes these drawings are rapid sketches to try out ideas, and sometimes they are detailed "studies" to get a good idea of how something will look in the finished work. The drawing above shows the same complex bending figure that it appears Van Gogh used in the painting (left).

Looking at Pictures

Many art museums encourage children as well as adults to enjoy them to the full. Some of the larger museums even have their own education department.

Pictures are all around us. We see them not only on the walls of art museums and other buildings, but also reproduced in books and magazines and in packaging and advertisements.

There are many different types of picture. They vary in subject and style and also in the purpose for which they were made. Today, many people paint as a hobby—simply for the pleasure it gives them. In the past, however, most pictures were painted for a specific purpose—to commemorate a famous man or woman or a great event, for example.

Paintings communicate many great people and events. John Trumbull, who painted this portrait of Thomas Jefferson, fought in the Revolutionary War against Britain and did many pictures that are valuable records of this period.

Below: Trumbull's most famous picture is this depiction of the signing of the Declaration of Independence. He painted most of the portraits in it from life and took more than ten years to finish the picture.

Left: *Mona Lisa* by Leonardo da Vinci is probably the most famous picture in the world. No one can be sure exactly who the model with the mystical smile was.

Below: *Rialto* by Antonio Canaletto (1697-1768). Canaletto worked mostly in Venice where he tried to reproduce the particular quality of the light on the canals and buildings of the city in his paintings.

Right: **This portrait by Ercole de Roberti, a 15th century painter is of a prominent nobleman patron, Giovanni II Bentivologlio.**

Below: *The Birth of Venus* **by Sandro Botticelli (1445-1510). Mythological themes were often commissioned by rich patrons of the Renaissance period in Italy.**

The most popular subject in Christian art is the Virgin Mary with the baby Jesus. This tender picture is by the 17th-century Italian painter Carlo Maratta.

Below: **This picture by an unidentified artist of the 16th-century, shows another very common subject in Christian art—Jesus's body being taken down from the cross to be laid in the tomb.**

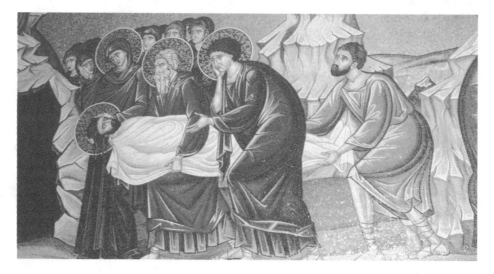

For many hundreds of years, almost all painting in Europe was on religious subjects, especially the life of Jesus. This was because religion played a very large part in everyone's life. In the Middle Ages, the village church was often the only stone building for miles around. It was the center of the community and people took great pride in decorating it. In other parts of the world, too, religion has often been the major subject for artists.

This painting is by the famous 15th-century Italian artist Sandro Botticelli, whose style was very graceful. He has shown Mary and Jesus accompanied by beautiful angels.

Below: **Francesco Bassano, a 16th-century Italian artist, painted this picture of Noah building the Ark. The story is told in Genesis, the first book of the Bible.**

Some of the oldest works of art that are known are paintings on the walls of caves in France and Spain made about 15,000 years ago. They mainly depict animals, and some people think that they were made as part of religious or magical rites. The cave dwellers depended on animals for food and clothing. Perhaps they held ceremonies in front of their animal paintings, hoping that their rites would help them to catch their prey.

Today, landscapes and still lifes are perhaps the most popular types of picture. These have been favorite subjects with Chinese painters for many hundreds of years, but in Europe they did not become popular until the 17th-century. By this time, artists had realized that the everyday world was full of interesting things to paint.

Opposite top: **Prehistoric cave painters had only very limited tools and materials, but they succeeded brilliantly in depicting the spirit and energy of the animals they hunted. This picture found in caves in Lascaux, France was painted about 20,000 years ago.**

Opposite below: **Prehistoric paintings of the human figure are normally less lifelike—more diagrammatic—than those of animals.**

Right: **This still life called *Roses, Dahlias et Lilas* was painted by Moise Jacobber in the 19th-century. It is typical of the very life-like Dutch still life paintings of the period.**

Chinese painters often had a great love of nature. They liked to show people in perfect harmony with the landscape.

Paintings of the everyday world are often the easiest to understand and like. However, even when we do not know the subject of a painting, we can often appreciate the artist's skill. A picture of St. George and the Dragon, for example, can be tremendously exciting, even if we do not know the details of the story. It is fun to find out such details, and the more you know about pictures, the more you are likely to enjoy them.

St. George is one of the saints who is most often represented in paintings. He is the patron saint of England and also of several Italian cities, including Venice where this colorful and energetic picture was painted by Tintoretto in the mid 16th-century.

Gabriel Metsu, who painted this charming scene, was one of the many 17th-century Dutch painters who specialized in pictures of everyday life.

Below: **The 18th-century British artist William Hogarth created a new type of everyday life picture. He painted scenes in a series (rather like a comic strip) to tell a moral story. This is the first of six telling the story of a marriage made for money rather than love.**

What Makes a Picture?

Some pictures are small enough to hold in the palm of your hand. These "miniatures" are usually portraits—often keepsakes of a loved one. Other paintings are so large that they cover whole walls or ceilings in churches or palaces. An artist who paints very small pictures will generally use lots of fine detail. An artist who paints very large pictures, however, will often use bold shapes that show up well from a distance.

Above: **Samuel Cooper, who painted this charming oval portrait, was one of the best British miniaturists of the 17th-century. This miniature is reproduced here at about its real size. Many miniatures were worn in pieces of jewelry such as lockets.**

Left: **This is the head of Ezelcial from the ceiling of the Sistine Chapel in the Vatican in Rome, Italy. Michelangelo painted his figures strongly and boldly because he knew that they had to stand out when seen from the floor about 50 feet (15 meters) below. It took him four years to paint the ceiling (1508-1512).**

The lines, shapes, and colors in a picture help to produce the effect or mood that the artist wants to create. Horizontal lines—going straight across the picture—help to suggest calm. They remind us of a flat, still landscape. Vertical (upright) lines can

This picture, called *The Surrender of Breda,* is by the great 17th-century Spanish artist Diego Velázquez. It commemorates a victory of the Spanish army, which had successfully beseiged the Dutch town of Breda. Velázquez contrasts the orderly upright forest of Spanish pikes on the right with the more bedraggled Dutch weapons on the left.

Below: **The strong horizontal forms of this landscape by John Constable called *La Vallata di Stour*, suggest peace and tranquillity. John Constable was one of the greatest British landscape artists of the 19th-century.**

The 19th-century French artist Edgar Degas was famous for his pictures of ballet dancers. He often based his paintings on photographs to give them a lively, unposed, "snapshot" quality.

Below: **This portrait by Rembrandt of his father displays a masterly use of oil paint. He has painted several layers of almost transparent color to gain a wonderful glowing quality to the picture.**

suggest strength and alertness, reminding us of soldiers on parade or the columns of a building. Diagonal lines suggest movement. Of course, artists do not use only straight lines. Curved lines, too, can help to create moods and effects. Gently curving lines can suggest graceful movement, while jagged lines can create a sense of bursting energy.

Lines form the boundaries of shapes. Many shapes, too, help to create certain feelings. Softly rounded shapes are often found in pictures of gentle subjects. Harsh, spiky shapes, on the other hand, can suggest tension or fierce emotions.

Colors often play a very important part in the impact of a painting. A soft green can have a soothing effect; it reminds us of a peaceful landscape. Bright red, on the other hand, suggests danger or violence; it is the color of blood.

Artists sometimes use colors symbolically. For example, the Virgin Mary is usually shown in pictures wearing a blue robe. This is because blue is the color of the sky, and she is regarded as the Queen of Heaven.

Some artists think hard about the lines, shapes, and colors in their pictures. They like to analyze things and try to understand how they

The Virgin and Child with Saints by Giovanni Bellini, a great Venetian artist who worked in the late 15th-and early 16th-centuries. He has shown the Virgin Mary in a traditional blue robe.

work. Some of them have even written books about such subjects as color or proportion. Other artists, however, prefer to follow their instincts.

Everyone sees things in a slightly different way. If twenty artists sit down to paint the same view or person or object, they will produce twenty different pictures. Each picture will show something of the personality of the artist who created it. One picture might be bold and energetic, for example, while another might be more timid but beautifully finished. We can recognize the styles of different painters, just as we can recognize the handwriting of different people.

Claude Monet (1840-1926) painted this beautiful picture of a *Woman with a Parasol*, in 1886. Monet was one of the leading members of the French Impressionist group of artists. The Impressionists were concerned with trying to reproduce the effects of sunlight upon color—their paintings usually have a wonderful intensity of color.

Right: **This oil painting by Bartolomé Murillo, a 16th-century Spanish artist, called *Peasant Boy Leaning on a Sill*, shows a very restrained use of color that creates a warm, subdued feel to the picture.**

Below: ***Still Life with Soup Tureen* by Paul Cézanne (1839-1906) shows a very different approach to the use of color from the Murillo picture. Cézanne was a member of the French Impressionist group of painters.**

Tools and Techniques

Most of the pictures you see in art museums are painted in oil colors on canvas. Oil paint is so popular because it is so versatile. The artist can use it to paint with bold, rough strokes of the brush or with very fine detail. Canvas, too, is very versatile. It is light in weight and can be cut to any shape or size.

Oil paint and canvas became popular in the 15th-century. Before then, artists had usually painted their pictures on stiff wooden panels. Instead of mixing their colors with oils, artists used the yolk of

This is a religious picture of a type known as an icon. The name comes from a Greek word meaning "likeness" and an icon is usually a very straightforward image of a saint or other holy person. Icons were mainly produced in Greece and Russia and were intended to help and inspire people in their prayers. Icons were usually painted on wooden panels.

This fresco shows the Virgin Mary with the body of Jesus after he had been taken down from the cross. It was painted by Giotto di Bendone in about 1305. Giotto was one of the first great Italian fresco painters. His pictures are still well preserved today.

eggs. This kind of paint is called egg tempera. Tempera paintings could be very beautiful, but they are hard to produce. The artist had to work slowly, using lots of tiny brushstrokes, because it was hard to blend colors. No wonder that oil paint took over!

When you buy oil colors today, the paint comes in little metal or plastic tubes. This kind of tube was invented in the 19th-century by an American painter called John G. Rand. It made oil paint more versatile than ever. Before this, many artists made their own paint, grinding up the raw materials needed to make the colors. If they bought paint ready-made, it

Before the invention of the metal tube, artists often bought oil paints in little sacks or bladders.

The French Impressionist painter
Claude Monet had a boat specially
fitted so he could paint on the river.
His friend Edouard Manet painted him
at work in 1874.

Watercolors like this
can easily be painted
out of doors because
the paint dries quickly.
This picture, called *A
River Landscape,* was
painted by Alfred
William Hunt (1830-
1896). He was a
prominent member of
the Royal Watercolor
Society in London.

came in little sacks. These had to be pricked to let the paint out and they were hard to reseal. The tube made it possible to carry oil paints around easily, so the artist could work out of doors. This was very important to the French Impressionists, who loved to paint landscapes in the open air.

Artists also paint pictures on paper. For this they usually use watercolor. As the name suggests, this uses water instead of oil or egg to make the paint flow. The paper usually shows through the thin, diluted color. This can produce very delicate effects.

This is part of a fresco painting showing events in the life of St. Peter. It was painted by the great Florentine artist Masaccio in the 1420s. The heads have great character and dignity.

Left: *The Reverend Robert Walker Skating* by Sir Henry Raeburn, a Scottish painterof the 19th century. The strong, dark, diagonal shape made by the figure gives the feeling of movement.

Below: **J. W. M. Turner (1775-1851) was a fine watercolor painter. In the latter part of his life he used similar techniques with oil paint, using many layers of transparent color to build up vibrant glowing colors. This picture called *The Fighting Temeraire* is a fine example of his atmospheric style of oil painting.**

The Laughing Cavalier by Frans Hals (1585-1666). Hals was an outstanding Dutch painter who specialized in portraits. He paid great attention to the intricate detail of the clothes worn by his subjects.

The Bar at the Follies Bergere was painted by Edouard Manet in 1882. It was his last great work. The mirrored image of the girl is an unusual aspect of the composition.

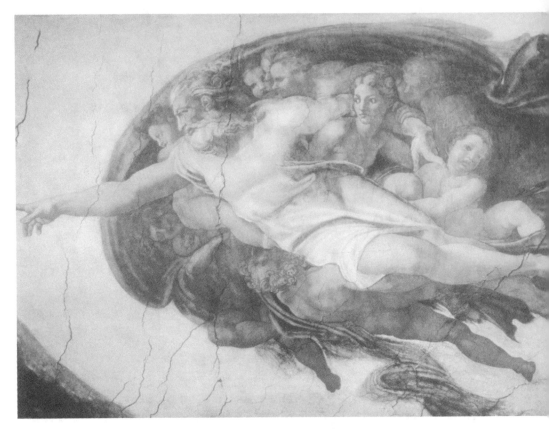

This is one of the most famous scenes from Michelangelo's ceiling of the Sistine Chapel. It shows God creating Adam. Almost all Michelangelo's paintings were done in fresco.

Watercolors are usually fairly small. At the opposite extreme are paintings that cover whole walls or ceilings of buildings. The main technique for this kind of painting is called fresco. This word is Italian for "fresh." The name comes from the fact that the artist paints on fresh wet plaster. When the paint dries it becomes part of the structure of the wall and does not flake off. Frescos are therefore very durable and can last in good condition for many centuries.

However, fresco has an enemy—dampness. If moisture gets into the wall, it can easily ruin the painting. Because of this, fresco has been used mainly in countries that have a warm, dry climate. Most of the really famous frescos are in Italy. Michelangelo's ceiling of the Sistine Chapel in Rome is probably the most famous of all. There are also many fine modern frescos in Mexico—a hot, dry country.

Modern artists have experimented with new types of paint. The

The British artist David Hockney painted this portrait in acrylic in 1970-71. It shows two of his friends who had recently married and their cat Percy.

most important type is called acrylic. Acrylic is mixed with water but it is almost as versatile as oil paint. Artists began using acrylic in the 1940s, and many painters now prefer it to oil.

Artists have used a great many materials to make drawings, including pens, pencils, charcoal, and chalk. Some of these materials have a very long history. For example, we know that the ancient Romans used charcoal, which is made from charred twigs or sticks. Artists still use it today, particularly if they want to produce a soft, blurred effect. The Romans also used pens with metal nibs, but until the 18th-century most pens were quills, made from the feathers of birds.

The type of pencil that we use today dates back to the 1790s. We call them "lead" pencils, but in fact they use graphite (a form of carbon) rather than lead. The graphite is mixed with clay and the amount of clay determines how hard or soft the pencil is.

Prince Balthazar Carlos on his Pony by Diego Velasquez, a Spanish artist of the seventeenth century. Velasquez was a master of oil painting.

Below: *The Stonebreaker* by Georges Seurat. Seurat (1859-1891). A French Impressionist painter, Seurat made many studies of color theory and the properties of color.

At the End of the Day The warm glow of evening sun is reproduced in this study by Jules Breton, a French painter of the 19th century.

Maurice Utrillo (1883-1955) painted this picture called *The Boulevard de Clichy under Suarr*. He is most well known for his paitings of Parisian street scenes.

Many artists make drawings directly from nature such as this pencil study of trees by John Constable.

Below: **This Van Gogh drawing of trees is in pen and ink. It is rougher in texture than the delicate Constable drawing.**

Edgar Degas often used pastels, especially late in his life when his eyesight was failing and they were easier to handle than oil paints.

The French painter Odilon Redon used pastel to create rich but delicate color effects.

This collage is by the German artist Kurt Schwitters (1887-1948) is simply called *Mirror Collage*. Many modern artists have produced collages from time to time, but Schwitters was one of the few artists to make it his main type of work.

Chalks, crayons, and pastels all come in sticks of color. Chalk is made from soft stones. Crayons are made of powdered color mixed with a waxy substance. Pastels are similar but made with gum or resin. Pictures made with pastels are sometimes classed as paintings and sometimes as drawings; they look like paintings, but because they are made without any kind of liquid, they are produced more like drawings.

Another type of picture is called a collage. This is made by pasting cut-out pieces of paper, scraps of material, or other bits and pieces onto a flat surface such as a sheet of paper or cardboard. The name comes from the French word "coller," which means "to gum." Many people who make collages like to cut photographs out of newspapers and then rearrange them into a new kind of picture, sometimes with amusing results. Collage began like this in the 19th-century as a kind of children's game, but in the 20th-century, many serious artists have experimented with it.

Make a Picture of Your Own

The tools and materials of the artist are very important, but the person who makes the picture is even more important. Every time you paint or draw a picture, you tell something about the kind of person you are. You tell something, too, of how you are feeling when you make the picture.

If you are happy, your picture may be different from the one you will make if you are sad or angry. Next time you make a picture, look at it and see if you can tell what it is saying about you. Some people like to make pictures of real things they can see in front of them. Others like to depict things that they remember or imagine.

Do you live in the country? If you do, many of the things you see and do belong to the countryside. If you make a picture of a country scene, your picture will show that you are drawing or painting something you know.

Your picture will tell where you live. It may tell, too, about the time in which you are living. A picture of the country today will be different from a picture of the country years ago when there were no tractors in the fields.

A boy or girl from the city can make a picture of the country, too, as they saw it on vacation or as they imagine it. Their pictures will be different from your picture of the country. The things they choose to draw or paint will probably be different. The way they see things will probably be different, too.

New Ways of Seeing

Artists work in many different styles, and many great painters have been unpopular at first because their work seemed strange and hard to understand. Until the early 20th-century, however, even the most adventurous artists painted subjects that everyone could recognize. In about 1910 this changed, because artists began painting pictures that were made up purely from lines and shapes and colors. This is called abstract art.

No single artist invented abstract art. A number of artists, in several different countries, all arrived at similar ideas at about the same time. They thought that forms and colors could be beautiful in themselves and did not have to represent anything.

Abstract painters work in many different ways. Some of them apply the paint with great energy, producing very exciting pictures with explosions of color. Others are cool and calm in approach. One of the most famous abstract artists was the Dutch painter Piet Mondrian. His paintings are so "pure" that he allowed himself to use only the "primary" colors (blue, red, and yellow) plus black and white. All his shapes have right angles. His paintings have no

Opposite: **Kurt Schwitters made most of his work from refuse such as bus tickets and bits of string.**

Left: **The Dutch painter Piet Mondrian was one of the most famous and influential abstract artists. Many other artists imitated his severely geometrical style.**

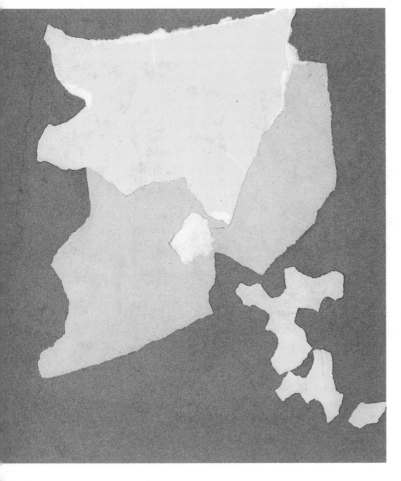

The French artist Jean Arp worked in anabstract style very different to that of Mondrian. He liked fluid, curving shapes rather than straight lines.

curved lines or any blending of colors. At first people found his pictures very strange, but gradually they saw that they had an austere beauty of their own.

Abstract painting became less popular in the 1930s, but a great revival took place in the late 1940s. This revival took place mainly in New York City, where a group of exciting young artists worked. They were called Abstract Expressionists. The most famous of them was Jackson Pollock, who created a completely new style of painting. He laid the canvas flat on the floor and walked around it dribbling and splashing paint on it from all sides. Many people laughed at this type of "Action Painting" and mocked Pollock by calling him "Jack the Dripper."

However, he is now regarded as one of the most brilliant and original painters of the 20th-century. It was mainly because of him and the other Abstract Expressionists that New York City became the world's most important center of contemporary art. Previously, Paris had been the place where all young artists wanted to go, but now New York was the most exciting place to be.

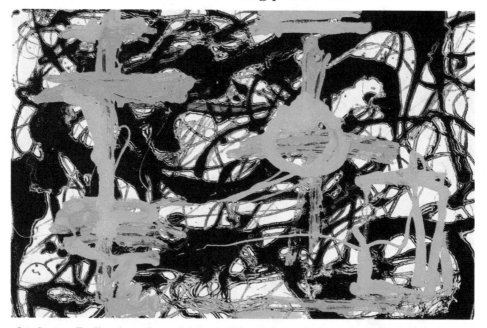

Jackson Pollock painted his "drip" pictures in a state of almost trancelike rapture. He sometimes used sticks, trowels, or his hands rather than brushes to apply the paint, and he sometimes mixed sand or broken glass with it. This picture, which he painted in 1948, is called *Yellow, Gray, Black*.

Not all famous 20th-century painters are abstract artists. Many of them have painted recognizable objects, but they look at things in new ways. The most famous 20th-century artist is the Spaniard Pablo Picasso. In his pictures he often distorted people's poses and expressions. By doing this, he emphasized the points he was trying to make.

Many 20th-century paintings are hard to understand at first, but it is often worth making an effort to look hard at them. If you find this kind of painting ugly or silly, don't worry. Some modern painting is ugly or silly, just as some old painting is pompous or boring. No one should expect to like all sorts of painting equally, and you should never pretend to like something that you actually dislike. But even if you dislike modern painting now, perhaps in a few years' time an abstract painting will catch your eye and you will think it is worth looking at this kind of painting again.

Pablo Picasso, the most famous artist of the 20th-century, often distorted his figures to express powerful emotions, as in this picture of a crying woman.

Paul Gauguin was one of the greatest French painters of the 19th-century, but he was poor and neglected for much of his career. He lived for several years in Tahiti and was one of the first European artists to appreciate the art of "primitive" people.

This portrait was painted by Amedeo Modigliani, an Italian who spent most of his career in Paris. His elegant, elongated forms are highly distinctive. As with Gauguin, his genius was not generally recognized until after his death.

Francis Bacon was one of the most famous of 20th-century British artists. His paintings are often disturbing for he painted people in isolation and despair.

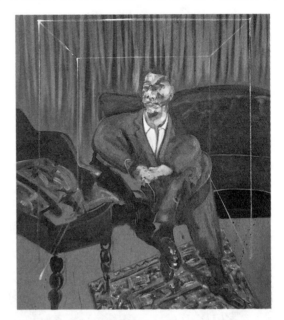

Unlike Francis Bacon, the Swiss painter Paul Klee generally had a cheerful outlook. His pictures often have a sense of almost childlike innocence.

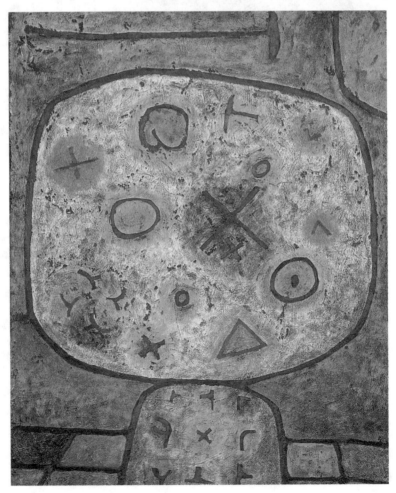

Prints

The 17th-century Dutch artist Rembrandt was the most famous of all etchers. He is said to have taken small etching plates out into the country with him, so he could make landscape etchings on the spot. This enabled him recreate accurately the scenes and effects of light and shade that interested him.

Making Multiple Pictures

The printing press for making books was first used in Europe about 550 years ago, in the middle of the 15th-century. Previously, single books had been written individually by hand, which was a very slow and laborious process. The printing press enabled multiple copies to be made from metal type. At about the same time, artists began to experiment with ways of producing multiple copies of pictures, using the same principle as book printers. They cut a design into a flat surface of wood or metal, applied ink to this, and then pressed it against a sheet of paper so that the design was transferred to the paper. The resulting picture is called a print.

There are many different kinds of print. The earliest ones were made by highly skilled craftsmen. They used sharp tools to cut the

The printing press was one of the most important inventions in history. It revolutionized the way in which knowledge was spread.

design into metal plates or wooden blocks. In addition, they had to remember an important point. When you take a print from a surface, the design that appears on the paper is reversed from left to right compared with what is on the plate or block. It is like looking in a mirror. So, if an artist wanted to include his signature as part of the print, he had to cut it back to front. Try signing your own name back to front!

The artist who engraves on a wood block usually holds the sharp tool away from the body and uses the other hand to steady or turn the block. .

About 50 years after printmaking was invented, someone thought up a brilliant time-saving method called etching. In this technique, the metal engraving plate is first covered with a thin layer of wax. The artist draws on the wax with a fine pointed tool called an etching needle. This is much easier than forcing a sharp tool through metal or wood. When the artist has finished the design, the metal plate is put in a "bath" of acid. The waxy coating on the metal plate resists the acid, but where the etching needle has scratched through the wax the acid eats into the metal. This process transfers the design to the plate. When the design is properly "bitten" into the plate, the artist removes the plate from the acid, cleans off the wax and makes a print by inking it in the normal way.

In etching, the artist can use very fine and delicate lines. The strength of the lines depends partly on how long the plate remains in the acid, and the artist can vary this to achieve different effects.

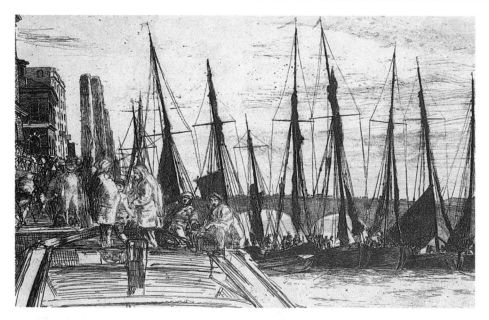

Prints can vary greatly in character. The etching by the American artist Whistler, above, is a subtle, sketchy impression of a quayside scene. The lithograph below, however, is a detailed, accurate record of the Bank of England in the 19th-century.

Etching is therefore a more subtle technique than ordinary engraving. The most famous of all etchers was the great 17th-century Dutch artist Rembrandt. The American painter James Whistler, who lived in the 19th-century, was another superb etcher.

Etchings and other kinds of printmaking are usually in black and white, but some artists make color prints. These are produced by exactly the same principle, but there is a different wooden block or metal plate for each color. Japanese artists are famous for their skill in making color woodblocks.

This print shows the beauty and subtlety of color that Japanese artists achieved with woodcuts.

Many other methods of making prints have been devised. Some of them are simply variations on the types already described. Other methods, however, show novel ways of thinking. One of these methods is called lithography. The name comes from the Greek words *lithos*, meaning stone, and *graphein*, meaning to write. As this suggests, the technique involves writing or drawing on stone.

The stone is a flat, smooth block. The artist draws on it with a greasy, waxy ink or crayon and then wets the stone. Grease repels water, so the parts of the stone with ink or crayon marks on it do not become wet. Next, greasy ink is rolled over the stone. It sticks to the parts that have the artist's design on it, but not to the parts where the water has been absorbed by the stone. Now a print can be taken from the stone by pressing a sheet of paper against it. The great advantage of lithography is that the artist can draw very freely, as if using a normal pen or crayon. Lithographic prints often have soft, subtle shading rather than the firm, hard lines of engraving.

This clever method was invented in 1798 by a German called Alois Senefelder. He was not an artist by profession, but a playwright who was experimenting with cheap ways of duplicating his plays. The idea came to him when he jotted down a laundry list on a piece of stone that happened to be lying at hand. He realized that the invention had great potential and published a book on it in 1818. It soon became very popular with artists. Usually the artists did not do the printing themselves, as this required expensive equipment.

This portrait of the actress Marilyn Monroe was made by the American artist Andy Warhol using the silk-screen process. Warhol liked to use very strong, gaudy colors.

This still-life by Pablo Picasso shows the very striking effects that can be obtained even with such simple printmaking methods as linocut.

Another ingenious method was invented in the early 20th-century. It is called silk-screen printing. In this technique, the artist works on a surface of fine silk mesh stretched over a frame. The artist creates a design by blocking off part of the mesh, either by painting opaque glue or varnish over it or by placing a stencil over it. Ink is rubbed over the silk with a kind of sponge, and it is squeezed through the fine mesh onto a sheet of paper below. At first, silk-screen printing was used mainly for printing patterns on textiles. However, artists began to experiment with it in the 1930s, and it was made very popular by the American Pop artist Andy Warhol in the 1960s.

You do not need special or expensive equipment to enjoy making prints. A very simple method is linocut. This is popular for teaching art in schools, because the material used—a thick sheet of linoleum—is much cheaper and easier to cut than metal or wood. However, some important artists have also used linocut, including Henri Matisse and Pablo Picasso.

Sculpture

This abstract work, *Hill Arches*, is by the famous British sculptor Henry Moore. It is made of bronze. Like many of Moore's sculptures, it was made to be displayed out of doors in a landscape

What is Sculpture?

Like drawing and painting, sculpture is something we can look at and see. But sculpture is different from a drawing or painting. It is solid. If it is a large figure, you can walk around it and see how different it looks from every point of view. If it is small enough, you can pick it up and turn it about in your hands.

Sculpture is made from clay, metal, wood, stone, or other materials. You can touch it and feel the coolness of the clay, the grain of the wood, the smooth or rough texture of the stone. Like drawing and painting, sculpture can express how the artist feels about things or people he knows, remembers, or imagines.

The Trevi fountain in Rome was built in the mid 18th-century. Rome is famous for its fountains and this is one of the most splendid in the city. The sculptured figures are placed in a very grand architectural framework.

Statues of the Buddha (the founder of Buddhism) play a great part in the art of the religion. He is usually shown in a very serene pose, sometimes sitting, sometimes standing or reclining.

This modern sculpture in Los Angeles is completely different in spirit from the Buddha statue. Rather than being still and awesome, it is energetic and carefree.

A World of Shapes

Sculpture has an even longer history than painting. The earliest sculptures that we know were made about 30,000 years ago. They are little figures of women, small enough to be held in the hand. No one knows why they were made, but perhaps they had some religious or magical significance.

Sculpture is also incredibly varied. It can be as small as a pebble or carved from something as big as a mountainside—like the famous heads of Presidents at Mount Rushmore in South Dakota. It can be made of something as heavy and solid as stone or of materials so light that they sway in the breeze. It can be part of a

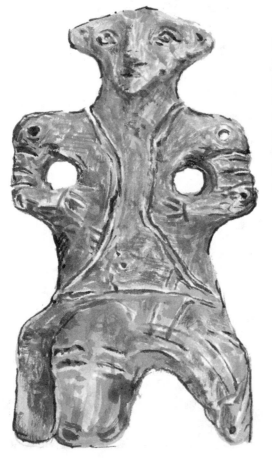

Many ancient people made little figures of the human body such as this, Usually we do not know their exact purpose, because they were made before the days of written records.

Mount Rushmore in the Black Hills of South Dakota. The American sculptor Gutza Borgun created the giant heads of Presidents Washington, Jefferson, Lincoln, and Theodore Roosevelt. He used dynamite and pneumatic drills to "carve" the stone. The work was sponsored by the US Government and took eleven years to complete (1930-41).

building or other structure, or it can stand alone. It can be rough-hewn or smoothly polished. It can be brightly painted or left in the lovely natural colors of stone or wood.

Most of the famous sculptures you see in art galleries are made of either marble or bronze, which are beautiful but expensive materials. They can survive in good condition for hundreds and even thousands of years. Many other materials are not so durable unless they are carefully preserved. Wood, for example, tends to rot. However, we can see many wonderful types of wood sculpture, including African masks and the totem poles made by various native American tribes of the northwest coast.

Totem poles were made by a number of Native American Indian tribes along the Pacific coast from southern Alaska to Washington state. These examples were made by the Tlingit tribe in the 19th-century (the photograph was taken in 1883). Totem poles were used as memorial columns, as grave markers, and for other purposes.

Like drawing and painting, sculpture changes as the way we live changes. Sculptors express new ideas in their shapes. They try to use shapes in new ways. They try to use new materials. Some sculptors today use scrap metal, including crushed automobile bodies. Other sculptors like to make shapes that move. These are called mobiles. They are made of wire and very thin sheets of metal. Sometimes they are powered by electric motors, but usually their movement is caused simply by letting them sway in the natural currents of air.

The American sculptor Alexander Calder invented a type of moving sculpture called a "mobile" in the 1920s. Sometimes they were moved by motors, but usually just by natural currents of air.

Bill Woodrow is one of a number of British sculptors who made their works from a bizarre assortment of rubbish and household articles.

Below: **This statue in the harbor in Copenhagen, Denmark, commemorates a story about a mermaid by Hans Christian Andersen, Denmark's most famous writer.**

This wooden mask typifies the bold, lively shapes seen in the sculpture of the Native American tribes of the Pacific coast.

These carved wooden poles are in Fiji, an island country in the South Pacific. Most native sculpture in this part of the world is made of wood, because it is more plentiful than stone or other suitable materials.

Modeling Figures from Clay

Clay is a wonderful material for making sculpture because it is so easy to work, and such fun to handle. You can push clay this way and that. You can squeeze it and pinch it. You can poke holes in clay to make eyes. You can scratch details and make a grinning mouth.

You can make a shape from one lump of clay, or you can take another lump of clay and push the two lumps together. You can add as many lumps of clay as you need to build your figure.

Clay remains easy to shape as long as you keep it moist. As it dries, it hardens, and you can keep a clay figure for a long time. You can make the clay still harder by baking it in the sun or in an oven called a kiln. Clay that has been "fired" in a kiln is called terra cotta, which is Italian for "baked earth."

You can paint clay figures, or you can make them bright and shiny by covering them with a glaze mixture and then baking them in a kiln.

Sculptors do not usually use clay for their finished works, because even when it has been hardened it remains fragile. However, they often use clay figures as models for sculptures in other, more long-lasting materials. Sometimes they make small models to get a feeling for the design before working on a large scale, and sometimes they make full-size models, take a mold from it, and use the mold to make a cast in bronze or other metal.

The clay models have to be as sturdy as possible, so sculptors use a kind of skeleton of wire fixed firmly on a base. This skeleton is called an armature. Sculptors then take lumps of moist clay and cover the skeleton as they build up the figure. When the rough figure is finished, they add details using tools made of wood and wire.

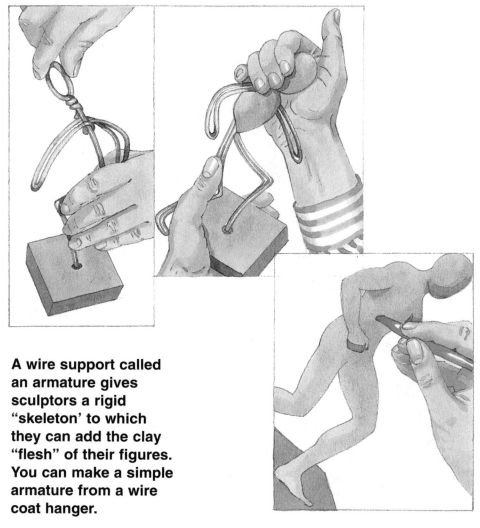

A wire support called an armature gives sculptors a rigid "skeleton' to which they can add the clay "flesh" of their figures. You can make a simple armature from a wire coat hanger.

Carving in Wood and Stone

Wood and stone are not like clay. You cannot twist or squeeze or model them into different shapes. Instead of adding more and more bits of clay to build up a figure, you have to remove material from the block of wood or stone that you start with. Carving is therefore often more difficult than modeling. If you make a mistake or change your mind when modeling in clay, you can simply start again, using the same material over again. But if you carve off too much wood or stone, you can't put it back again.

The simplest form of woodcarving is whittling on a stick. All you need for this is a knife. You can also use a knife for carving figures in softwood, such as white pine. If you use a harder wood, like walnut, you need a gouge and a straight-edge chisel, and a mallet with which to hammer.

When the figure is done, you can smooth away the rough edges with sandpaper. Then you can spread a light coating of shellac over it. You can sand it with a fine-grained sandpaper, and polish it with wax until it has a shiny gloss.

Many diferent kinds of wood can be carved. Hard wood is more difficult to work than soft wood, but it can be carved with greater detail.

Stone is harder to carve than wood, and because good stone is also heavy and expensive, it is used only by professional artists.

Sculptors have used many different types of stone, from granite, which is extremely hard and difficult to carve, to alabaster, which is comparatively soft. Granite is most suitable for large outdoor memorials that do not require fine detail. The ancient Egyptians used it for some of their most impressive statues. It can be polished to a beautifully smooth surface. Alabaster has been used mainly for small indoor sculptures. It was very popular for little altarpieces in the Middle Ages.

The favorite stone for sculptors is marble. Some of it is pure white, but it is also found in many other colors. The texture also varies. Some of it can be carved to a very smooth and sleek surface. Other kinds are more crystalline with a beautiful sparkle.

Top: **This delicate little carving is typical of the alabaster altarpieces that were made in great numbers in the Middle Ages. The city of Nottingham in England was well known for making such pieces, which were exported to many European countries.**

Left: **A building in Venice richly adorned with sculpture and carving.**

This marble statue of St. Matthew by Michelangelo is unfinished. The figure seems to be "emerging" from the block of stone.

This Egyptian granite figure of a sphinx has been badly damaged in places, but granite can often survive in extremely good condition.

Photography

This dynamic image has been created by computer manipulation of a photograph. It looks rather like an "op art" painting, underlining the fact that photography is a world in which art and science meet.

Creating Pictures with Light

For hundreds of years, prints were the only kind of multiple copy pictures that could be made. This changed in the 19th-century when photography was invented. The first photograph was taken in 1826 by a Frenchman named Joseph-Nicephoré Niépce. It was a view from a window in his house. The exposure took eight hours because his materials were much less sensitive to light than the ones we use today. The photograph Niépce took is dim and blurred, but he had made history.

In the next few years, another Frenchman named Louis Daguerre, continued Niépc's experiments. In 1839, he announced that he had created a photographic process in which the exposure took only about a minute and produced incredibly sharp detail. People were amazed by the results and one painter exclaimed in dismay "From today painting is dead!"

But the "daguerreotype" had drawbacks. The photo-

This daguerreotype photograph was taken in about 1850. People had to pose for several minutes while the exposure was made.

graph was produced on a copper plate that had to be handled very carefully to avoid damaging the picture. Also, this picture was unique; it could not be duplicated.

However, in the same year that Daguerre announced his invention, an Englishman named William Henry Fox Talbot made the next great advance. He invented the negative, from which any number of prints can be made. This is the basis of photography as we know it today.

Right: **The English physicist William Henry Fox Talbot (1800-77) was one of the most important figures in the history of photography. He invented the negative, and in 1844 published the first book to be illustrated by photographs.**

Below: **Fox Talbot seen here with a group of his friends.**

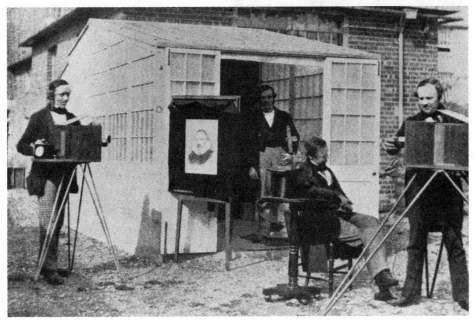

Within ten years, photography had spread all over the world. Because of this, we can see in photographs almost all the great people and events of the second half of the 19th-century. For example, Mathew Brady made thousands of photographs of the American Civil War. He employed a team of twenty photographers. They used traveling darkrooms in covered wagons so that the delicate photographic negatives could be developed before the emulsion dried. Each negative was on a single large glass plate. By this time, exposures took about ten seconds, so photographers still had to be content with static subjects.

Many advances in technology have helped to make the kinds of cameras and films we use today. For example, experiments were made with color photography in the 19th-century, but it was not until the 20th-century that successful processes were invented. The first "snapshot" camera was sold by the Kodak Company in 1888. It was called the Kodak Brownie. This camera was sold with a roll of film already inside, and the whole camera had to be sent off to the factory for the film to be developed. The Polaroid camera, which produced a print within a minute of taking a picture, was first available in 1948.

Mathew Brady's photographs give us a detailed record of the Civil War. This one shows a field hospital in about 1865.

Art or Science?

This photograph of crystals viewed through a microscope was taken for scientific purposes but it creates an intriguing abstract pattern.

Ever since the invention of photography, people have argued about whether it is an art or a science or both. The sensible answer is that it is both. Photography can be a highly technical subject, and modern cameras are marvels of electronic and engineering skill. Specialized cameras can take pictures anywhere from outer space to inside the human body. Some of them work so quickly that they can photograph a bullet as it is fired from the barrel of a gun.

Most of us use cameras simply to take family snapshots, to preserve our memories on paper. Billions of these simple photographs are taken every year. The pictures taken by serious photographers are very different in spirit. The most creative and skillful photographers express their personalities vividly in their work. We can sometimes recognize the style of a great photographer almost as easily as we can recognize the style of a great painter.

Photographers can make simple objects look interesting or startling simply by using their imaginations. By moving the camera during the exposure, the photographer created a kaleidoscope-like pattern from this panel of colored lights.

Photographers vary as much or even more than painters in their choice of subject. Some of them like to work in a studio where they can control the light, making it harsh or soft or changing its direction to create dramatic shadows or bring out the texture of objects. These photographers may spend hours setting up a shot to get every detail perfect.

Other photographers like to capture scenes on film as they happen. A great part of their skill lies in choosing the decisive moment to release the shutter. For many photographers, the creative work does not end when they have taken the picture. Some photographers take pride in producing their own prints in the darkroom so that they can bring out every subtlety of tone and texture. Some like to experiment in the darkroom, using various techniques to alter the image.

Types of Cameras

There are many different types of cameras in use today. Some of them are made for special purposes such as filming underwater, but most of them can be used in many different situations. The most common way of classifying cameras is by the size of film they take. There are some beautifully made and very expensive "miniature" cameras (similar to the ones you sometimes see in spy movies when someone is secretly filming documents). However, the smallest size in general use is called 110 format. In this format, the film is 16mm wide and comes packaged in a plastic cartridge that drops directly into the back of the camera. Because it is so simple to load and handle, it is very suitable for young children to use and for taking basic snapshots. The drawbacks of the 110 format are that it is not very versatile—on most cameras you cannot change lenses—and that because of the small size of the negative, the prints you get are also rather small (if you enlarge them, they begin to look grainy).

35mm cassette

110 cartridge

Next up in size is the 35mm format, so-called because each frame of the film measures 35mm wide. This is the most popular type of film with both professional photographers and serious amateurs. If you are really interested in taking good quality photographs, you will almost certainly use a 35mm camera.

This format is so popular because it is so versatile. The film size is big enough to be able to produce high-quality enlargements, but small enough for the cameras to be light and easy to carry. Camera manufacturers make a huge range of lenses and accessories for 35mm cameras, so they can be adapted for almost any purpose. Usually the manufacturers concentrate their research and development on these cameras, so they are always at the forefront of technology. Film manufacturers, too, realize that this is the most important part of the market, so they also concentrate much of their effort on finding ways to improve 35mm film.

Modern 35mm single lens reflex (SLR) cameras are so versatile that they can be used for taking almost any kind of picture. The lens can be changed to get a different angle of view and filter, like those shown below can be added to the lenses to create special effects.

The simpler 35mm cameras have a fixed lens, but one of the main reasons for owning a more complex model is that you can change lenses and therefore bring greater variety to the type of photographs you take. The "standard" lens that usually comes fitted to a new camera gives a view that corresponds pretty closely to the way we ordinarily see the world. If you fit a wide-angle lens to the camera, it takes in a broader view. This type of lens is therefore useful if you want to photograph a subject that will not fit within the viewfinder when you are using a standard lens. For example, you might be inside a room and find that the standard lens shows too small a part of it. If you cannot step back any farther (perhaps because there is a wall behind you) a wide-angle lens is the solution.

shutter release button

mirror

A cutaway diagram of a modern 35mm single lens reflex camera. It is so-called because the image to be photographed is seen through the viewfinder via a mirror that reflects the light coming through the lens. The mirror flips up out of the way when the shutter release is pressed allowing the light onto the surface of the film.

interchangable lens

A long-focus or telephoto lens works in the opposite way. It is just like a telescope or pair of binoculars, enabling you to get a closer shot of something that is too far away for a standard lens. Both wide-angle and telephoto lenses can greatly increase the enjoyment you get from photography. However, they have drawbacks. One is that they can be very expensive: the huge lenses used by professional sports photographers to take close-ups from the sidelines cost many thousands of dollars. Another is that such lenses can introduce distortions to the picture. You can see this at its most extreme in photographs taken with "fisheye" lenses. These are the ultimate in wide-angle lenses; they can take in a 180 degree view (as if we could see out of the back of our heads as well as the front), but they make straight lines look curved. They can produce startling and exciting results, but they need to be used with skill.

Another type of lens that is often used with 35mm cameras is the zoom lens. In this kind of lens, the angle of view that it takes in can be varied, so one lens can take the place of two or three. Some cameras come already fitted with a zoom lens that varies from a moderate wide-angle to a moderate telephoto, covering most of the angles that you will use in general photography.

The next size up from 35mm is known as medium format. The film in this type of camera is usually 6 x 4.5cm, 6 x 6cm, or 6 x 7cm. This means that each frame is roughly four times the area of a

frame of 35mm film. Because the film has to be enlarged less, it can show more fine detail. The drawback is that medium-format cameras are larger, heavier, and more expensive than 35mm models. Consequently, these cameras are used by photographers to whom a high-quality image is more important than portability or versatility. Fashion photographers, for example, often prefer medium-format cameras to any other type.

Medium-format cameras do not have the enormous range of lenses and accessories of 35mm cameras, but many of them have interchangable backs. These backs are light-tight magazines containing a roll of film. Often, fashion photographers take a preliminary shot using a back containing Polaroid film, so that they can immediately check to see what the final result will look like. Then they simply change to a back containing ordinary film to take the final shot itself. In the same way, a photographer can easily switch from black-and-white to color film without having to change cameras.

The biggest cameras in normal use are called large-format or view cameras. These take single sheets of film rather than the rolls of film used in smaller types. Sheet film comes in various sizes, the most common sizes including 4 x 5 inches and 8 x 10 inches, the largest size in normal use. Large-format cameras take a long time to set up and operate, so they are used only by photographers who want to obtain the highest possible image quality and can spend a lot of time on each shot. The glossy pictures you see in magazines advertising food and other products are usually taken with large-format cameras. Outside the studio, large-format cameras are mainly used by architectural photographers. These cameras are able to correct the distortions in perspective caused by lenses.

This photograph of solar panels was taken with a "fisheye" lens, which takes in a very wide angle of view.

Using Cameras

Modern cameras are so cleverly made that you need never worry about getting pictures that are in focus and properly exposed. Most of the cameras made for beginners do this automatically. A light-sensitive cell in the camera measures the brightness of the light and adjusts the aperture (the opening through which light passes through the lens to the film) so that neither too little nor too much light enters the camera. If too little light enters, the film will be underexposed and the picture will look very dark. If too much light enters, the film will be overexposed and the picture will look pale and washed out.

At the same time (on many cameras), the lens adjusts so that the subject is in focus. This is usually done by means of a beam of infra-red light (which we cannot see) being emitted from the camera and bouncing off the subject back to the camera. Electronic devices in the camera can then calculate the distance to the subject and adjust the lens accordingly. The closer the subject is, the greater the distance between the lens and the film has to be, so if your subject is near, the lens on an automatic focus camera will project out a little farther than if you are photographing a distant subject.

These adjustments happen so quickly—in the time it takes you to blink—that you do not have to think about them. If you want to find out more about how your camera works, it is a good idea to open the back (when you have no film in it!) and watch what happens inside when you press the shutter release button. Depending on what kind of camera you have, you may be able to watch the aperture opening and closing. In very bright light, it will open up only a little way for a fraction of a second. In very dull light, it will open wider and/or longer.

It is an exciting thing to have a camera for the first time. But even though today's cameras can perform these marvelous feats of auto-

Spot the Dolphin! This photograph illustrates clearly why you should usually try to get close to your subject. The leaping Dolphin that should be the center of attraction is tiny compared with the boring foreground and muddled background.

matic, virtually instantaneous adjustment, many people are disappointed when they have their first film developed. What often happens is that the thing or person you photographed seems very small on the print, with lots of unwanted foreground and background. This is because when you concentrate on looking at something, your brain tends to filter out the surroundings that do not interest you. However, the "eye" of the camera does not work like this. It sees everything in front of it with the same clarity, so unless your subject fills a large part of the area of the frame, it can look swamped by the surroundings.

Another common fault is to take a picture of someone and

This photograph makes two points about how you need to "see" with the camera's eye. The child at the left is cut in half by poor framing and the man appears to have a rock growing out of his head.

not notice that there is a lamppost or something similar in the distance directly behind them; when you get the picture, it looks as if there is a post growing out of the person's head! So you need to think about everything that is included in the viewfinder, not just your immediate subject. If you take pictures regularly you soon learn to do this. Often it is a good idea to try to get a plain background behind your subject, so that it stands out more clearly. When professionals are taking photographs in the studio, they use large rolls of colored paper for this purpose.

This moody evening scene shows how a picture can look good even if there is very little in it. Everything depends on the subtlety of the lighting.

Automatic cameras are almost foolproof, but they have a disadvantage. They ensure that you get a properly exposed, well-focused picture, but they do not allow you to make decisions of your own about the picture. That is why professionals and serious amateurs use cameras in which they can adjust the exposure and the focus themselves (these are usually called "manual" cameras, or sometimes automatic cameras have a "manual override," meaning that you can switch off the automatic features and control focus and exposure yourself). For example, you might want the foreground of your picture to be clearly focused but the background to be blurred. With a manual camera you can do this easily, whereas with an automatic camera, everything is usually equally sharp. If you are taking a picture of a landscape, you might decide that it would look more moody and romantic if the colors were paler. You can achieve this effect simply by deliberately overexposing.

From Home Movies to Videos

Still pictures are not the only type of picture that can be made at home by the amateur. Cameras are available for making moving pictures in color. At first, people used small hand-held movie cameras to make home movies. Then, in the 1980s, the video camcorder became widely available for people to make color home videos, which they could then play on their videocassette recorders (VCRs). This is much easier than setting up an old-fashioned home movie projector to play a reel of film. Many people now use camcorders to make videos of vacations, weddings, parties, and other special occasions.

The VCR has become very popular as a way to view rented movies at home on the television set, to record television programs that are broadcast at times when it is inconvenient for you to watch them, and to view home videos. Sony Corporation of Japan started selling the first widely available VCR in 1969. VCRs use a cassette of magnetic tape to record both picture and sound, and camcorders record moving pictures onto a videocassette tape.

Whether using an old-style movie camera or a camcorder, the biggest challenge to the maker of moving pictures is the same: unless you use a tripod or are able to move the camera around smoothly, the resulting film will be very jumpy as you point the lens toward different subjects.

Video cameras can also be used by professionals to take still pictures onto small magnetic discs. The discs can electronically store many images in a small space. These images can then be printed, shown on a computer monitor or television screen, or sent over telephone lines to a distant location.

John Coltraine was one of
the leading jazz
saxophonists of the 1960s.

Music

What Makes Music?

Music consists of sounds arranged in patterns. These patterns are usually made up of groups of notes that are repeated and often subtly varied as the piece of music goes along. There are various kinds of patterns in music. The most important are melody, rhythm, and harmony.

Melody is simply another word for tune. It is a succession of notes that form a rising and falling pattern. Rhythm is the beat of music—a pattern in which some notes are stressed more than others. It can be fast or slow, steady or fluidly changing. In some music the beat is very strong; in other types of music we are hardly aware of it, but it still provides a framework for the notes. Harmony is a word used to describe several voices or instruments singing or playing together so that their different sounds complement one another rather than clash.

Good Vibrations

All sound is made up of vibrations in the air. The vibrating air causes tiny movements in our eardrums, and our brains interpret these as sounds. Different instruments (and voices) produce different kinds of vibration and therefore different kinds of sound.

There are several different ways of producing the vibrations that musical instruments make. The simplest way is by striking something. Instruments that we play in this way are called percussion instruments. This group of instruments includes anything that can be banged or shaken to make a musical noise. Most percussion instruments, such as drums and tambourines, do not produce specific notes; they are used to make rhythm. However, some percussion instruments can play tunes; the xylophone is an example.

The instruments on this page all belong to the percussion family. Only the glockenspiel among them can play tunes; the others are used for rhythm.

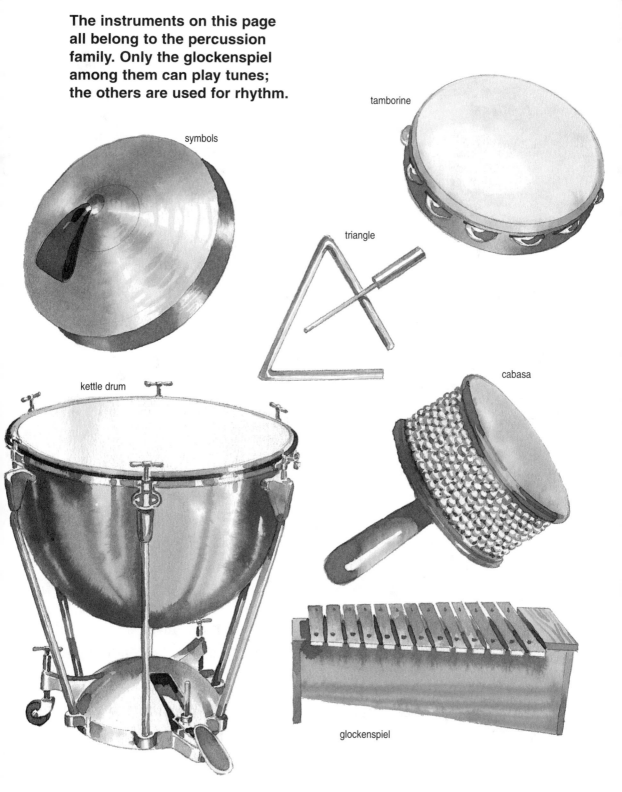

tamborine

symbols

triangle

cabasa

kettle drum

glockenspiel

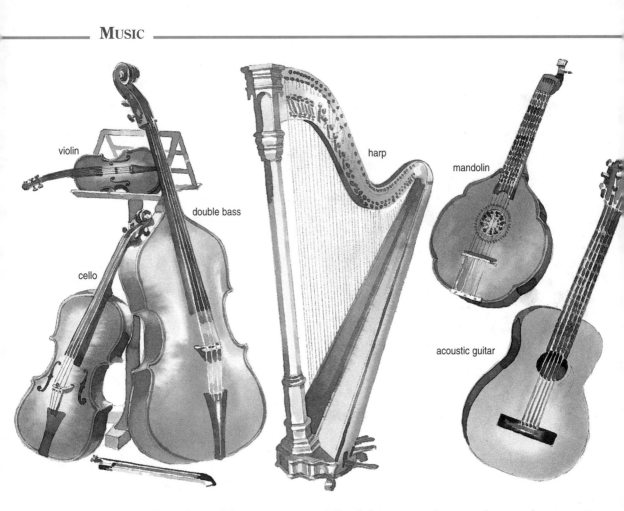

violin

double bass

cello

harp

mandolin

acoustic guitar

These are stringed instruments. All of them can be used as solo instruments or in combination with other instruments.

In stringed instruments, you either pluck the strings with your fingers, as with a guitar or harp, or rub a bow across them, as with a violin or cello. In wind instruments, such as a trumpet or oboe, you make the air move by blowing into them.

The fourth major group of instruments is made up of keyboard instruments, such as the piano and harpsichord. In these instruments you press a key that sets off a mechanism that causes a small hammer to strike or pluck a string.

Organs are also keyboard instruments, but they create sounds in a different way, usually by pumping air through a series of pipes.

All these instruments have been known for hundreds of years, but in the 20th-century, new instruments have been created by making sounds electronically. Some of these new instruments are common instruments whose sounds are amplified electronically.

The best-known of this type of instrument is the electric guitar. In the electric guitar, the movement of the strings is converted into an electric current. This current can be altered in various ways by electronic circuits and then used to drive a loudspeaker. A non-electric guitar is now known as an acoustic guitar.

Another type of instrument produces sound entirely by electronic devices, such as electronic oscillators which produce a variety of sound waves. The synthesizer, which became popular with rock musicians in the 1960s, is the best-known example of this type. A synthesizer can take different forms, but it usually has a keyboard and various switches and other controls. As well as imitating the sound of other instruments, it can alter sounds in various ways and also create new ones.

Electric guitars and electric keyboards are among the principle instruments used in modern pop music.

The Beginning of Music

There is a kind of music in nature. The waves of the sea are always moving, and they make high or low sounds, beating out a rhythm as they break against the shore. The wind makes a whistling noise as it moves through the branches and leaves of trees. Many kinds of birds make noises that we find pleasant; we say that they sing.

When and how did people begin to make music? No one knows for sure, but many people have ideas about the beginning of human music. Some people think it started with singing; other people think that it started with beating time.

Perhaps a cave man shouted with pride when he killed a mammoth. Later he shouted again as he told his people of his victory. His shouts made a kind of song. Perhaps he stamped his feet as he

Music began in prehistoric times. Perhaps the first "musicians" were cave men who shouted a kind of triumphal song to celebrate their success in hunting

shouted his victory song. The beat of his stamping made a kind of crude rhythm.

The first musical instruments were probably hands clapping together and feet beating time. Today we still clap our hands to the beat of a song. Our feet still beat time to the exciting rhythm of a march or a dancing tune.

Later, perhaps, someone hollowed out a log and stretched the skin of an animal across it. This was the first drum. Or someone took a hollow grass stalk and blew through it. This was the first wind instrument.

The ways in which we make music have changed greatly since those far-off days, but some of the kinds of music are still the same. Mothers have always sung lullabies. A cave mother had no words or language. She could not sing a tune, but her soft grunts made a sleepy song that a cave baby could understand. A baby of today could understand it, too, because a lullaby is comforting music that makes a baby feel safe, protected, and loved.

A lullabye is a soothing song to lull a baby to sleep. The 19th-century German composer Johannes Brahms wrote probably the most famous of all lullabies. It is known simply as "The Brahms Lullabye."

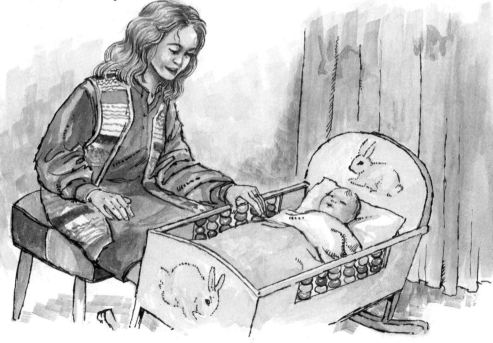

The Troubadours

In the early days of history, few people could read or write, but they still had stories to tell. Many times, they sang their stories. The Vikings of Denmark and Norway were bold sailors and fighters. They sang songs to tell stories of sea battles or of Viking heroes. These story songs traveled from country to country. A sailor from Norway might sing his song in an Irish town. A sailor from Denmark might sing his song in England or France.

The people of England and France and other countries made story songs, too. There were no magazines or newspapers to tell the news in the 10th, 11th or 12th centuries. There was no radio or television. But just like you, people wanted to know and tell the things that were happening. They made songs to tell the news.

Traveling musicians, called troubadours or minstrels, sang and played on their harps as they went from country to country. They sang true stories of heroes and battles. They sang sad stories and funny stories. They played and sang in the castles of kings, in village squares, and in country inns. They sang stories of their own and stories they had heard others sing. Some of their songs have survived to the present day and can be heard on recordings of medieval music.

Sometimes famous men liked to compose their own songs as well as listen to those performed by troubadours. King Richard the Lionheart of England, who lived in the 12th-century, loved music and wrote songs. Only one of his songs survives today, but several by his favorite troubadour, a Frenchman called Blondel, are still known today.

There is a famous story about Richard, Blondel, and their songs. When Richard was captured by one of his enemies, Blondel is said to have traveled through Europe trying to find out where he was imprisoned. As he went, he sang one of their favorite songs. One day he heard a voice from a castle window singing an answering verse and he knew he had found his master. We do not know how much truth there is in the story, but Richard was certainly held captive, and the song that survives by him was perhaps written during this time, because it is about being a prisoner.

Folk Songs

People liked to listen to the troubadours sing just as you like to listen to recordings, or to songs on radio or television. People liked to sing themselves, too. Sometimes they sang the songs they had heard the troubadours sing. Many other times they made up songs of their own. We call these songs folk songs. Because they were sung by ordinary people rather than by professionals and because they were not written down, folk songs are usually fairly simple, with a single, clear melody. Many can be performed with the voice alone, without any kind of instrumental accompaniment. Sometimes the same tune is used for several different songs.

We do not know who first made up these folk songs. We do not know in which country some of these songs were first sung, because some folk songs seem to travel all over the world.

As the songs traveled, they changed, so that the same song was sung just a little differently in different places and in different times. People loved singing the songs and passed them on to their children and grandchildren. People remembered the songs, but they did not always remember them in exactly the same way. Today, we sing many folk songs that were first sung in other countries hundreds of years ago. We do not sing them exactly as the people of the time sang them. If you hear the song in one place, it may sound just a little different from the way people sing it in another area or country.

Sometimes the folk songs of a people reflect their history. During the American Revolutionr, the British soldiers sang a song to tease the American soldiers. The Americans laughed and began singing the song themselves. When the British surrendered at Yorktown in 1781, the Americans sang that same song. It was "Yankee Doodle."

People have always made songs to sing as they marched or played or worked. Cowboys of the old West sang as they rounded

The famous American song "Yankee Doodle" seems to have first been sung in about 1740. The words were first printed in the 1760s and the music in the 1790s. These musicians are depicted in a painting by A. M. Willard called *The Spirit of '76*.

up the cattle. They sang as they watched the herds at night. It kept the cattle quiet and helped to pass the time. Sailors sang as they raised sail or pulled up anchor. The rhythm helped them to work in unison, as they all heaved on the same beat.

Sailors' work songs are called chanties. The sailor who led the singing was known as the chanteyman, and he was regarded as a very important member of the crew, because if he was good at leading the singing he could get the work done more quickly. People used to say that "a good chanteyman is worth four extra hands on the rope." He had to know how to spin a song out with extra verses if the work took longer than expected. One of the most famous chanties is called "Blow the Man Down." There are many other chanties, mainly sung by British and American sailors. They were popular until steam powered vessels replaced sailing ships in the late 19th and early 20th centuries.

The pioneers in covered wagons sang songs as they made their way slowly across the great plains to California. The men who laid the railway tracks across the vast continent sang songs as they worked. One of the most famous songs of this type is called "I've been Working on the Railroad." The first verse goes like this:

I've been working on the railroad,
All the livelong day,
I've been working on the railroad,
Just to pass the time away.

These songs are part of the history of the United States. Like the people of America, the songs have come from many far lands. They have traveled north, south, east, and west until they now belong to all of us.

In about 1900, people began collecting these old songs and writing them down and putting them in books. They knew that if people stopped singing a song it would be forgotten. Sometimes they found a song in a logging camp, a mining camp, or at a rodeo or a country square dance. They wanted these songs to be remembered because they help tell the story of the building of their country. Other people sang these songs and made records of them, so we could all hear and learn to sing them, too.

Some of the most famous folk songs were originally work songs. The regular repeated rhythms helped people such as sailors and railroad workers do their labor in unison.

Writing Music

When people started collecting folk songs, they were able to write down the tunes as well as the words on paper. The letters of the alphabet and the symbols we use to write music are each kinds of codes. Before you learn to read words or music, the signs look like meaningless patterns on the page. Once you have learned the codes, you can understand the messages they contain and start writing your own.

The ancient Greeks devised a way of writing down music, but it was forgotten for centuries. It was forgotten so completely that in the seventh-century a scholar wrote: "Unless sounds are remembered by man, they perish, for they cannot be written down." About three centuries after this, however, some monks invented a new way of writing musical notes, and this is still the basis of the system we use today. The monks wrote down the musical sounds, or notes, by putting lines and dots together.

The lines run parallel across the page in an arrangement called a staff or stave. Each line, and each space between the lines, represents a particular level, or pitch, of highness or lowness of sound. The higher a note is on the staff, the higher its pitch.

The system that we use for writing music today was invented about 900 years ago. There have been many changes to it since then, but the essentials remain the

Each note is given a letter from A (the lowest) to G (the highest), and after these seven letters, the sequence is repeated from A to G again. The distance between a note and the next highest or lowest note with the same letter is called an octave.

Originally the monks wrote music only for church choirs, but the system they invented was so successful that other people found they could adapt it to write down any type of music, for any voice or instrument, or for any combination of instruments. Each voice or instrument could be given its own staff when the music was written down.

Ludwig van Beethoven (1770-1827) was one of the greatest and most versatile of all composers. His hearing began to fail when he was about 30, and by the time he was 50 he was completely deaf. However, he continued to write wonderful music for the rest of his life, even though he could never hear it himself.

The Orchestra

Musical instruments play together in many different combinations. For example, two violins, a viola, and a cello form a string quartet. Many great composers have written music for this combination.

The largest combination of instruments is the orchestra, which sometimes includes as many as a hundred players. It was not always this big, but developed to this size during the 17th, 18th, and 19th centuries.

The instruments of the modern symphony orchestra usually follow a standard layout, arranged around the conductor in an arc, with violins to his left and cellos and double basses to his right.

The first orchestras consisted only of stringed instruments. Then oboes and bassoons were added. Later, flutes and clarinets came in. Now the orchestra had a woodwind section. Composers wrote music for the stringed instruments and the woodwinds to play together.

Sometimes a pair of trumpets and a pair of kettledrums played with the orchestra. The blare of trumpets and the beat of drums were stirring sounds! This was the beginning of the brass and percussion sections of the orchestra. Then the brass section grew until it had trumpets, horns, trombones, and tubas.

The conductor/composer John Williams leads the Boston Pops Orchestra in rehearsals. The conductor can make his instructions to the musicians clearly understood by signals he makes with his baton.

As the orchestra grew in size and played more complex music, the musicians found that they needed someone to act as director, to make sure that all their different instruments blended into a pleasing sound. This person became known as the conductor. The conductor is sometimes compared to a general leading his troops or to a master chef who blends many ingredients into one delicious dish.

Today the conductor usually directs the orchestra using a short stick called a baton. Before the baton became popular in the 19th-century, conductors used various other objects for this purpose. Some used a roll of paper, for example, and some used a violinist's bow. The 17th-century French composer Jean-Baptiste Lully used to beat on the floor with a big stick. This method of conducting caused his death, because one day he accidentally struck himself on his foot with the stick and the wound turned gangrenous!

Sir Thomas Beecham was one of the greatest conductors of modern times. His recordings are still considered to be some of the finest ever made.

Great conductors can inspire the orchestra in such a way that they produce a distinctive sound for them. People who are very interested in classical music and listen to it a lot can often recognize a particular conductor even if they are played only a short passage of one of his recordings. It is very difficult to describe how conductors achieve their effects, but all great conductors have very strong personalities that come out in their work.

Two of the most famous of all conductors were the Italian Arturo Toscanini (who lived in America for much of his life) and the Englishman Sir Thomas Beecham. Their personalities came out very strongly in their music-making. Toscanini had what we think of as a typical Latin temperament; he was very intense, with a volcanic temper. His performances have enormous fire and energy. Beecham, on the other hand, was suave and charming, almost as famous for his witticisms as he was for his conducting. Many of his performances have an exquisite lightness and grace.

Musicians loved playing for Beecham, because he had such style and charm, even though he could be unpredictable. A player in an American orchestra being conducted by him once said: "Any guy who can turn up fifteen minutes late for a T.V. show sponsored by Kellogg's Corn Flakes and just explain on the air that he had lost a button in the hotel is the man for me!"

Toscanini died in 1957 and Beecham in 1961, but their recordings still sell in large numbers today, even though modern recordings have much better sound quality. Many people think that some of their recordings are unlikely ever to be surpassed.

Symphonies and Concertos

Orchestras play many different kinds of music, but two types are particularly popular—symphonies and concertos. If you go to a concert by a famous orchestra, there will probably be either a symphony or a concerto among the works it plays. Possibly there will be one of each.

A symphony is a fairly long work in which the whole orchestra plays a part, although not all the instruments play all the time. There are usually four sections, or movements, in a symphony. The first movement usually goes at a moderate or fairly fast pace, while the second is generally slow. The third movement is often in a lively dance rhythm, and the fourth movement is usually fast and energetic to bring the work to a stirring conclusion.

Symphonies became popular in the 18th century, and some of the finest composers of the time wrote dozens of them. Haydn wrote more than a hundred, for example, and Mozart wrote about forty. Most of the great composers of the 19th-century also

In the 18th century, orchestras such as this played symphonies and concertos written by composers such as Haydn and Mozart.

Beethoven

wrote symphonies. These were often longer and more complex than those written in the 18th-century, so the 19th-century composers usually did not write so many as their predecessors. Beethoven wrote nine symphonies, for example, and Brahms wrote four.

The concerto is a work composed for orchestra and a solo instrumentalist. Piano concertos are the most common type, and there are also some very popular violin concertos by great composers, including Beethoven, Brahms, Elgar, Sibelius, and Tchaikovsky. Concertos have also been written for numerous other instruments, including the cello, clarinet, and horn. One of the most popular pieces of 20th-century music is the guitar concerto by the Spanish composer Joaquin Rodrigo.

Sometimes composers write concertos for two or more solo instruments. Brahms wrote a "double concerto" featuring a cello

These three composers are (left to right) Beethoven, Tchaikovsky, and Mozart. Their symphonies and concertos are among the most frequently performed and recorded works of orchestral music.

Tchaikovsky   Mozart

and violin, and Beethoven wrote a "triple concerto" featuring a cello, violin, and piano.

Most concertos are in three movements. The middle movement is usually slow and often rather dreamy; the two "outer" movements are quicker, with the final one sometimes being very fast and exciting. Often the part for the solo instrument is extremely difficult, so only brilliant musicians can play it well. Some composers have themselves been superb soloists, and their concertos gave them a chance to show off their skills. Sergei Rachmaninov, for example, was one of the greatest pianists of the 20th-century as well as one of the greatest composers. Fortunately he made recordings of all four of his piano concertos with himself as soloist, so although he died many years ago, we can still hear the beauty of his playing.

Music and Drama

Music sometimes exists just by itself, as beautiful sound. But music is often combined with other art forms. When a poem is set to music, it becomes a song. When a number of songs are put together to tell a story, they form a kind of musical play. We call this kind of play an opera.

The first opera was presented in Italy around the year 1600. Soon composers were writing operas in France and Germany, too. The stories of early operas were usually taken from Greek and Roman myths. These operas were usually seen only by rich people, because they were expensive to produce. In addition to singers and musicians, they needed lavish costumes and scenery. Some wealthy aristocrats loved opera so much that they built their own private opera houses.

This scene from Mozart's *The Magic Flute*, produced by the English National Opera, shows the appeal of the sheer spectacle of opera, with lavish sets and costumes.

Opera is still an expensive art to produce, but if we do not get the opportunity to see it "live" we can still enjoy it on recordings or film. In 1990, three of the world's most famous opera singers gave a concert in Rome to celebrate the soccer World Cup final being played there. The singers were José Carreras, Placido Domingo, and Luciano Pavarotti. The concert was beamed all around the world by satellite and seen by millions of people. It was such a success that four years later, the "Three Tenors" did a similar concert in Los Angeles to celebrate the World Cup final there.

The "Three Tenors" have given some extremely popular concerts that have helped to bring opera to people who would normally not hear it.

The music in operas is of various types. There are choruses, in which many people sing together; and there are duets (for two voices), trios (for three voices), and quartets (for four voices). Sometimes characters have a conversation in song. However, the high points of most operas are solo songs in which the main characters express their feelings. These songs are called arias.

The feelings the singers express in arias are often very passionate, because many operas are based on tragic subjects. Often the hero or heroine dies at the end. However, there are also comic operas. These are sometimes called light operas. When such an opera has spoken rather than sung dialogue, it is often called an operetta (which means "little opera").

In the 20th-century, the operetta developed into the musical, in which a story is told through spoken words, song, and dance. The musical has become very popular in the movies as well as on stage. Musicals are often light-hearted, with an emphasis on spectacular costumes and scenery. There are also serious musicals, such as *West Side Story*, which is a modern version of Shakespeare's *Romeo and Juliet*, set in the United States rather than Italy. The music for *West Side Story* was written by the famous American composer and conductor Leonard Bernstein.

West Side Story was first performed on stage in 1957 and was made into a highly successful movie in 1961. The music is by Leonard Bernstein and the lyrics are by Stephen Sondheim.

The success of musicals has not meant the end of traditional opera. Modern composers still write operas, although few 20th-century operas have achieved the popularity of the great masterpieces of the past. However, even some of the greatest operas were unsuccessful at first. Georges Bizet's *Carmen* is now perhaps the most popular of all operas, but when it was first performed in 1875, most critics hated it!

Music and Dance

When we enjoy music, we often tap our feet in time with the beat or sometimes sway gently along with the tune. Dancing is a more elaborate way of moving along with music, in which we use our whole bodies. There are many different types of dancing, ranging from primitive war dances to sedate ballroom dancing, in which the men dress in white tie and tails and the women in glamorous dresses.

Ballroom dancing is performed by couples. The most popular dances include the waltz, polka and tango. Competitions are often held for both amateur and professional dancers.

Ballet began at about the same time as opera. Originally, ballets were not independent shows; they were part of other entertainments, including operas. Full-length ballets, making up a whole evening's entertainment, did not appear until the 19th-century. They were particularly popular in Russia, where Tchaikovsky became famous for his ballet music. He wrote the music for *The Nutcracker*, *Sleeping Beauty*, and *Swan Lake*, which are probably the three most popular ballets in the world.

Swan Lake, for which he wrote the music in 1877, was the first of Peter Tchaikovsky's great ballets. With his other masterpieces, *Sleeping Beauty* and *The Nutcracker*, it remains at the heart of the classical ballet repertoire.

We usually think of ballets as very elegant and graceful, but they are not all like this. In 1913, a ballet called *The Rite of Spring* was premiered in Paris. The music was by the great Russian composer Igor Stravinsky and the choreography was by Vaslav Nijinsky, who was the most famous male dancer in the world at this time. This ballet told a story of pagan Russia, and the music and the dancing were incredibly fierce and energetic. No one had seen or heard anything quite like it before. Some people were thrilled by it. Others hated it and started to boo or leave the theater. Fights broke out in the audience, and the whole event descended into chaos. It was one of the most amazing nights in the history of music or the theater. Now, *The Rite of Spring* is regarded as a masterpiece.

Vaslav Nijinsky (1890-1950) was the greatest male dancer of his era. He was famous for the sensitivity of his interpretations as well as for his athletic energy, especially in his spectacular leaps.

Everyone can manage to do some kind of dance, and anyone who is prepared to practice hard can learn ballroom dancing. But ballet is not for everyone. It requires years of serious training to make the body strong and supple enough to perform the movements with grace and perfect timing. A ballet dancer has to be a dedicated athlete as well as an artist.

Religious Music

Some of the most beautiful music has been written to be performed in churches. The type of religious music that you probably know best are hymns. These are songs that are sung by all the congregation in a church, usually accompanied by an instrument (in many churches this is an organ). Because everyone joins in, the tunes have to be fairly simple and easy to remember. The best hymn tunes are so good that once you hear them it is hard ever to forget them. Some of the most famous ones are "Amazing Grace," "Onward, Christian Soldiers," and "We Plough the Fields and Scatter."

Some hymns were written to be sung by the church choir alone, without the congregation. These are called anthems or motets. Because they are sung by trained singers, they can be more complex than ordinary hymns.

Another type of religious song is called a carol. In fact, this word can refer to any song of joy and thanksgiving, but we nearly always use it to describe the songs sung at Christmas to celebrate the birth of Jesus.

The oldest Christian hymns date back to about 400 AD, but some of the hymns of other religions are much older. Some hymns from India, written in the ancient language Sanskrit, are believed to date from around 1200 BC.

The spiritual is another type of religious song, which originated among black slaves in the southern United States. The words of spirituals often helped the slaves to draw comfort and inspiration from the Bible; in the Bible, the Israelites were enslaved by the Egyptians, but they escaped from it, just as the American slaves hoped to be freed. A collection of spirituals was published in 1867 with the title *Slave Songs of the United States*, and this book helped this type of music to become more widely known.

There are many other types of religious music. One of the most important is the oratorio. This tells a religious story in a way that is similar to an opera. There are solo arias, choruses, and an orches-

The black slaves of the Southern states of the United States sang religious songs called spirituals. These songs later influenced jazz and blues music.

tral accompaniment. However, unlike operas, oratorios are usually performed without scenery, costumes, or acted action. The most famous of all oratorios is *Messiah* by George Frederick Handel, a German-born composer who settled in England.

It was first performed in 1742 in Dublin and was an overwhelming success: one critic described it as "the finest composition of music that ever was heard." The following year it was performed in London. King George II is said to have risen to his feet during the most famous part of *Messiah*—the "Hallelujah Chorus"—because the music was so stirring and uplifting. The rest of the audience followed his example, and it became a tradition for the audience to stand during this part of the work.

Handel's *Messiah* became incredibly popular with choral societies, and in the 19th-century it was fashionable to perform it with choirs of up to 500 people. It must have been an overwhelming experience to hear so many people singing such sublime music. Now, however, the fashion is to use much smaller choirs. This brings a gain in clarity, but loses something in sheer impact.

Jazz

Music is constantly developing. Styles and fashions come and go. Some of these are quickly forgotten, but others leave a permanent impression. Jazz is one of the most original and lasting innovations in 20th-century music. It was created by black American musicians in the South (particularly in New Orleans), and from there it has spread all over the world. It is America's most influential contribution to the world of music.

It is easy to recognize jazz when you hear it, but it is difficult to define exactly what makes it jazz. There is a distinctive bouncy "swing" to the sound that comes from small departures from the regular rhythm. Jazz usually involves improvisation; the musicians start with a basic plan but make up ideas as they go along. The American composer, conductor, and pianist André Previn is one of the few musicians to have had equally successful careers in jazz and classical music. He summed up the difference between them like this: "The basic difference between classical music and jazz is that in the former the music is always greater than its performance—whereas the way jazz is performed is always more important than what is being played."

The first jazz recordings were made by the Original Dixieland Jazz Band in 1917, and soon after that, jazz began spreading all over the country, particularly to Chicago and New York. Before long it had spread to Europe, too, particularly London and Paris.

The earliest jazz bands usually had about seven musicians: three or four soloists backed by a rhythm section that set the beat. In the 1930s, however, "big bands" became popular, led by such famous musicians as Count Basie, Duke Ellington, Benny Goodman, and Glenn Miller. The sound of the big bands was usually smoother than that of the earlier jazz groups.

There are many other types of jazz, including bebop, which became popular in the 1940s. It is usually fast and energetic. There are also many famous jazz solo instrumentalists and singers with

**Glenn Miller (top) and
Count Basie (above at piano) were
leaders of two of the most famous jazz "big bands."**

their own individual styles. They include the pianists Dave Brubeck and Thelonius Monk, the saxophonists John Coltrane and Charlie "Bird" Parker, and the trumpet players Louis "Satchmo" Armstrong and Miles Davis.

Armstrong and Davis provide good examples of how jazz musicians can change and adapt the conventions of jazz music, and how difficult it is to pin down and define these conventions. Armstrong was one of the first great stars of jazz in the 1920s and was acclaimed for his superb and seemingly effortless technique on the trumpet.

Charlie Parker (1920-55), above, John Coltrane (1926-67), above right, and Louis Armstrong (1901-71), right, were three of the greatest jazz soloists.

Later, however, he moved more into films and popular entertainment, and by the end of his life (he died in 1981) he was as well known for his distinctive gravelly singing voice as for his trumpet playing. His hit records "Hello Dolly" (1964) and "What a Wonderful World" (1968) were more mainstream pop than jazz, and his warm personality gave him a strong appeal to people who were not interested in jazz as such.

Davis, too, had superb technical skill on his instrument. In the early 1950s, he turned from a fast, aggressive way of playing to a "cool" style for which he became famous and which influenced many other jazz musicians. Later he experimented with electronic instruments and with blending jazz with rock rhythms.

Blues and Soul

Jazz is not the only kind of distinctive music that grew up among black American musicians. The blues is the name given to a type of music that is sometimes similar to jazz but is somber in spirit. It deals with the sadness and disappointments of life and is sometimes very raw and emotional. It can be defiant, quiet, or meditative. The blues developed from various influences, including work songs and spirituals going back to the times when many black Americans were slaves.

Like jazz, the blues originated in the South. The style of music

Chuck Berry, born in 1926, is one of the most enduringly popular of rock singers. He had his first hit records in 1955 and was still touring more than 40 years later. He writes many of his own songs and has become famous for his witty lyrics as well as for his amusing antics on stage.

B.B. King, born in 1925, is one of the most famous blues musicians—he is a superb guitarist and a fine singer. He has influenced white as well as black musicians.

called rhythm and blues, however, developed mostly in the industrial cities of the northern states, such as Chicago, in the late 1940s. This blended the emotionalism of the blues with hard, driving rhythms. A typical rhythm and blues (or "R&B") band was made up of a rhythm section (usually consisting of drums and a bass guitar, or double bass and perhaps a piano) together with a soloist, usually a vocalist and/or guitarist. The leading stars of R&B included B.B. King and Chuck Berry. Their exciting music was one of the sources of rock and roll, which became fashionable in the 1950s.

Another type of music that is strongly associated with black performers, such as Aretha Franklin, and James Brown, is soul music. This can be similar to rhythm and blues, but has its own kind of intensity, often produced by an almost sobbing kind of vocal delivery. Many black R&B and soul performers such as the Supremes and Marvin Gaye, achieved great success in the 1960s with recordings on the Motown label, founded in Detroit in 1959. They became so popular that many white performers began singing in similar styles.

Popular Music

Popular, or "pop," music is perhaps even more difficult to define than jazz. It does not describe a particular style of music. The words can be used to refer to any music that has mass appeal. Usually such music is fairly simple and tuneful. Since the 1950s, the term has been particularly used to describe any music that is intended to appeal strongly to young listeners, especially teenagers. As teenagers became more independent and had more money to spend, record companies realized that they could make a lot of money by giving them their own music, different from the type their parents liked.

Elvis Presley (1937-77) was the most successful and influential solo performer in the history of pop music. He also became the star of many films.

Much pop music is called rock music, or rock and roll. This has a very strong beat and is suited to energetic dancing. The main instruments are electric guitars and drums. Some people like to play it at an extremely loud volume. Gentler types of pop music place more emphasis on melody. The words of the songs are often about falling in and out of love.

During the 1960s the Beatles were the most famous and popular musical act in the world. They could hardly be heard at their live concerts because of the screaming of their fans—this kind of adulation was called "Beatlemania."

A great deal of pop music is quickly forgotten, but some of it has shown lasting appeal. The American singer Elvis Presley sold more records than anyone else, and his songs are still extremely popular, long after his death in 1977. His admirers call him the "King of Rock 'n' Roll," or simply "the King." The most successful pop group was The Beatles, made up of four British musicians from Liverpool. They dominated pop music in the 1960s and split up in 1970. Today their recordings are still played and loved all over the world.

Country and Western

A lot of pop music is hard to classify, but there are also some fairly distinctive types. One of the most popular is country and western music (sometimes called simply "country music"). Like jazz, this originated in the southern United States. But while jazz belongs mainly to towns, country music—as the name suggests—was born in rural areas. Originally it was called hillbilly music ("hillbilly" being a slang term for a person from a backwoods area).

Hank Williams (1923-53) died very young of a heart attack, but he is regarded as one of the greatest figures in the history of country and western music. His son Hank Williams Junior is also a Country singer.

Dolly Parton, born in 1946, is one of the most popular country and western singers in the world today. She has also written many successful songs and has acted in several films.

Country music is hard to define exactly, but one of the most famous country singers—Hank Williams—gave a good description of its character: "Hillbilly singers sing more sincere than most entertainers because the hillbilly was raised rougher than most entertainers. You got to know hard work. You got to have smelled a lot of mule manure before you can sing like a hillbilly." It is the kind of music sung by cowboys, accompanied by a guitar, banjo, or fiddle. Songs are often about hard work or loneliness, as well as about the ever-popular subject of love. Singers often have a southern twang to their voice or try to imitate one.

Originally, hillbilly music was a genuine folk art, made by country people for their own enjoyment. It was first recorded in the 1920s, and by the 1950s was becoming popular all over the country, being broadcast on radio as well as played live. Today it often blends with other types of pop music, although some country performers like to keep it as authentic as possible. It is now also very popular in many countries outside the United States, and performers such as Johnny Cash and Dolly Parton are international stars.

Fashions in Pop Music

Fashions are constantly changing in pop music, and it is hard to keep track of all the new trends. Up to the 1960s, most other countries copied American music, but after the sensational success of the Beatles, British music became very popular all over the world, and pop became more international in flavor. Now the music of other countries sometimes influences American pop, although America and Britain still lead the world. Styles are constantly blending to create other styles. In the mid 1970s, for example, disco music became very popular; this was similar to soul music but had a heavily rhythmic beat.

The popularity of disco music was one of the reasons for the enormous success of the film *Saturday Night Fever* (1977), which starred John Travolta as a young man whose life revolved around disco dancing. A long-playing record of music from the film, performed by the Bee Gees, sold about 30 million copies. It is said to be the highest-selling record of the 1970s.

The film *Saturday Night Fever* featured music by the Bee Gees. Their album of the same name included such highly successful songs as "How Deep is Your Love,'" "Night Fever,'" and "Stayin' Alive."

The big stars of pop music are highly varied in their styles. Michael Jackson and Prince sing in the tradition of Motown and soul. Bruce Springsteen performs exciting rock music. Performers such as Barry Manilow and Barbra Streisand sing more melodic material. Many pop performers have brief careers, making headlines and one or two hit records and then quickly being forgotten. However, some of them have great staying power. The British group The Rolling Stones, for example, had its first hit record in 1963 but was still giving huge sell-out concerts more than 30 years later. The group's lead singer, Mick Jagger, is a terrific crowd-pleasing performer.

Barbra Streisand, born in 1942, and Prince, born in 1958, are two of the most individual performers in the modern pop music scene.

Bruce Springsteen, born in 1949 (top inset), Mick Jagger, born in 1943 (lower inset), and Michael Jackson, born in 1958, are three of the most exciting stage performers in the history of pop music.

This production of "Much Ado About Nothing," written by William Shakespeare, was directed by Franco Zeffirelli in 1965. Nineteenth century costume and set design rather than the dress of Shakespeare's era was used.

Drama

A Make-Believe World

It is exciting to see a play. The lights in the auditorium go out, the lights on the stage go on, and up there is a make-believe world where we can see and hear a story come alive. The people in the story laugh or cry, and we want to laugh or cry with them.

A play is like a magic carpet. It can take us to faraway lands or to a world that is just like our own street and town. It can take us to a world of the future, where people travel to distant planets, or it can take us to any time in the past. If the people in the play sail off on a ship looking for Treasure Island, we feel that we are sailing on that ship, too.

We share their adventures. We shiver with delighted excitement when young Jim Hawkins meets wily Long John Silver. Young Jim is our friend. We cower with him in the apple barrel as he listens to the pirates plotting. What will happen next? Will the wicked pirates be able to steal away the treasure?

That is the magic of the theater. It can take us into another world, and while we watch, that world is real for us. The people in the play are real, and we share their hopes and their fears.

Plays are often adapted from other forms of literature. Robert Louis Stevenson's exciting novel *Treasure Island* has been performed on the stage many times as well as in the movies and on television.

Early Developments

No one knows for sure when the first play was acted. However, according to legend, it happened thousands of years ago in Greece. At this time, the ancient Greeks used to perform a ceremony in which they sang and danced in praise of their god Dionysus, but no words were spoken.

Then, so the legend goes, a poet, called Thespis, acted the part of the god. When the people sang and danced, he spoke to them. They sang back their answers to him. This was the first time that dialogue was used in a play.

Some people did not like this new idea because it seemed strange to them, but many other people liked it very much. Ever since then, actors have talked to each other to help act out the story of a play.

We do not know how much of the legend of Thespis is true, but even today actors are sometimes called thespians in memory of him, and the ancient Greeks were certainly the first people we

know of who created great drama. They wrote both comedies and tragedies. Some of their plays are still performed today, and some of their theaters still survive. Most Greek theaters were open-air structures. They had banks of stone seats, and these were sometimes arranged around a natural hollow in the landscape, creating a lovely setting for the plays.

The Romans, like the Greeks, greatly enjoyed plays. After the collapse of the Roman empire, there was a gap of many centuries when the art of theater in the European world practically died. However, drama flourished in the Asian world.

For example, India's ancient literary tradition gave rise to Sanskrit-language plays as early as 200 BC. Most of the plays were based on epic narratives, traditional tales of love, magic, and rivalry involving Hindu gods or mythical characters. Not all Sanskrit plays were based on the ancient epics: some were original stories. Classical Sanskrit drama continued to develop for at least nine centuries.

Southeast Asia—including such places as Thailand, Cambodia, Vietnam, Myanmar (Burma), Java, and Bali—has a 1,000-year-old theatrical tradition that combines drama, music, dance, masks, and puppetry to create colorful and spectacular performances. Traditional plays focus on legends and mythical figures, and traditional detailed costumes are used to identify specific characters. Often, the actors improvise their lines.

The earliest plays in English were given in about the 13th-century. They were sponsored by the church authorities and were on religious subjects. Originally the plays were performed by priests to help people understand the stories of the Bible. At the time, priests were virtually the only people who could read and write. They performed the plays in Latin, which was still a living spoken language for scholars. Ordinary people could not understand the words, but they could follow the action because the stories were simple and direct.

The plays became so popular that they moved out of the church into the churchyard, where more people could see them. When the plays moved outside, they changed. They still told Bible stories, but the actors spoke English, not Latin. The characters in the plays began to sound like real people.

The priests stopped acting in the plays. Carpenters, merchants, and other working people formed their own acting groups. Each kind of worker had his own society, or guild. Each guild gave its own special play. For example, the shipbuilders' guild acted out the story of the building of Noah's Ark.

These plays are usually called Miracle Plays or Mystery Plays. The word "Mystery" does not mean that they were meant to be mysterious. It comes from the medieval French word *mestier*, which means "trade" or "profession."

Often guild actors gave their plays on a large wagon called a pageant. They moved this pageant from place to place and acted the play over and over, so all the people in the town could see it. Later, people began calling the play itself a pageant.

Today we have pageants of many kinds. A parade of floats on a holiday carnival is one kind of pageant. An outdoor play given to celebrate a special day in history is another kind of pageant.

In this medieval style pageant, statues of Jesus and the Virgin Mary are carried in procession around an Indian village as part of the Easter celebrations.

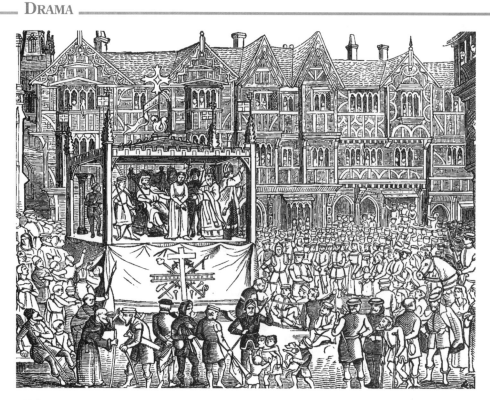

This illustration shows how a mystery play might have appeared being performed in a town square in the early 16th century.

Mystery plays died out in the 16th-century. All religious art declined in England at this time after King Henry VIII broke away from the Roman Catholic Church. But people began to write plays on other subjects. One of these people was William Shakespeare, the world's most famous playwright. He worked for a professional theater company and became a wealthy man, because his plays were very popular.

Many of the plays of William Shakespeare (left) were performed in the Globe Theater in London (right). This artist's impression gives a good idea of how it must have looked.

The theaters in which Shakespeare's plays were originally performed were usually open to the air and roughly circular in shape.
Spectators who could afford to pay for seats were in covered galleries. Poorer people stood in the open arena in the center of the
theater and looked up at the stage. Unfortunately none of the theaters built in England in Shakespeare's time still exists, although
the foundations of one in London were uncovered during building
work in the 1980s. A complete reconstruction of the Globe Theater
has been completed upon the original site. We know about their
appearance mainly from contemporary descriptions and illustrations. Using these descriptions and illustrations, some people have
made reconstructions of Elizabethan theaters. For example, there
is a very splendid Elizabethan stage in the Folger Shakespeare
Library in Washington D.C., which houses the world's greatest collection of Shakespearean books.

Stories on Stage

Words are the most important part of a play. The same play can be presented in different styles and costumes or even on the radio, so that we do not see anything at all, but the words remain the same. Some plays have scenes in which an actor talks alone, as if he or she is thinking out loud. This kind of speech is called a monologue or a soliloquy. Most of the speech in plays, however, is called dialogue, in which the actors talk to each other.

The words that the actors speak to each other help to tell the story of the play, but they also do more—they tell us many things about the people, or characters, in the play. The writer of the play tries to make the characters sound real and interesting, so that we believe in them and care about what happens to them. Usually the story, or plot, of a play can be summarized quite briefly, so what really matters is how the story is told.

The way in which a character speaks can tell us many different things about him or her. It can tell us where the character lives or comes from. A boy from Texas does not sound exactly like a boy from Maine. A girl from Iowa may not sound just like a girl from Georgia. Their accents are different, and some of the words they use are just a little different, too.

Dialogue also tells us at what time the character is living. If a play is set in the present day, then the characters will usually talk much

Opposite: **Many plays are adapted from other literary forms.** *Scrooge* **is adapted from "A Christmas Carol," a novel by Charles Dickens.**

Right: **This is an intensely dramatic scene from Shakespeare's** *Macbeth*. **The title character confesses to his wife, Lady Macbeth, after he has murdered King Duncan to gain the crown.**

as we do. If the play is happening in the times of King Arthur or Robin Hood or the American Revolution, then the writer will try to make the characters sound as if they belonged to those ages.

Dialogue tells us other things, too. It tells us about how the characters live and how they relate to one another. King Arthur will not speak like one of his woodcutters. A fisherman will use different words than a scientist. Just as you speak differently when you talk to a teacher than you do when you talk to a friend, so characters in a play speak in different ways according to the situation and mood of the story.

Voices change as feelings change. You speak quickly and jerkily if you are excited or angry. You speak slowly if you are tired. Listen to the voices around you. Even if the words are in a foreign language that you do not understand, the sounds of the voices can tell you if the people speaking are angry or sad or happy.

Actors do not use only their voices to tell the story of a play. They use their whole bodies to convey their feelings with gestures and expressions. An actor playing a character who is proud and vain will move in a way that is very different from an actor who is playing a humble or timid character. Skillful actors can even say one thing with their words but show with their expressions that they really think or mean something entirely different. An actor playing a villain sometimes has to appear to be charming on the surface but evil underneath.

Scenery
and Costumes

Although words are more important than anything else in the theater, plays can impress us through our eyes as well as our ears. Every play has a place and time where and when the action of the story happens. We call this the setting. How does a play show this? It tells it through the dialogue of the characters, and often, too, by the way the stage looks.

The stage can be made to show an inside scene, such as a living

room or a castle hall; or an outdoor scene., such as a mountainside or a sandy beach. These illusions are created using painted backdrops (called stage sets or scenery) and real objects, such as furniture or potted plants.

There can be pictures on the walls and chairs and tables and other furniture on the stage. There can be cookies and lemonade and other foods and drinks on the tables. Sometimes these are real and sometimes they are only pretend. All these things help to make the play seem more real. They are called the stage properties, or "props."

We can also use light to change the way the stage looks. In the 19th-century, people began using gas, instead of candles or oil lamps, to light the stage. Today we use electricity to make parts of the stage dark or bright. We use lights of different colors to create the effect of moonlight or sunlight, or to suggest an eerie atmosphere for the witches in Shakespeare's *Macbeth*.

Scenery, properties, and lighting can create a very realistic set-

This is a scene from a 1992 production of Noel Coward's play *Hay Fever*, which was first performed in 1925. A great deal of effort has been put into the set, costumes, and props to create a convincing 1920s atmosphere.

A scene involving the three witches from Shakespeare's *Macbeth* shows how lighting and make-up can be used to create a powerful, eerie effect.

ting for a play, but you do not have to use these things to make a successful play. Sometimes the audience can just imagine the setting. This is what used to happen in Shakespeare's day. His plays were usually performed in the open air in daylight, so they had no artificial lighting effects at all. The stage was a platform set out from one wall. Sometimes there were curtains with scenes painted on them to show the setting, but often only a simple sign was hung on the stage. It might say "The Castle" or "The Forest of Arden," and the imaginations of the people in the audience would have to do the rest.

In contrast to the scenery, the stage costumes of Shakespeare's time were often colorful and magnificent. The clothes that the actors wore were not usually meant to be realistic. When Shakespeare's company performed *Julius Caesar* or *Macbeth*, they did not try to find out what people had worn in ancient Rome or medieval Scotland. Instead, the costumes were intended to be appropriate to the individual characters, emphasizing the wearer's station in life or underlining some aspect of personality. Often there was symbolism in the color of the clothes. For example, purple was traditionally the color worn by royalty, and a somber gray-green called willow green was the color allotted to characters who were unhappily in love.

When a Shakespeare play is produced today, the costumes can be of various types. They can belong to the period in which the play is set, to Shakespeare's period, or to some other time. In a production of *Julius Caesar*, for example, the characters can be dressed in Roman togas and armor, in Elizabethan costume, or even in modern clothes. Many people prefer the older types of costume, but some modern-dress performances of Shakespeare's plays have been highly praised.

A great advantage of modern dress is that it is cheaper and easier to find. Some people also think that an old play can look more relevant to our own time if the costumes belong to the present day. On the other hand, dressing up in colorful costumes is part of the fun and excitement of the theater, and if the actors wear ordinary clothes, we lose some of the feeling of a special occasion.

This is a scene from a modern production of *The Importance of Being Earnest* by Oscar Wilde, which was first produced in 1895. The splendid costumes recreate the fashions of that time.

Make-up and Masks

Dressing up and applying make-up is all part of the fun children can have in putting on a play.

The costume that an actor wears can help the audience to believe in the character he or she is playing. In the same way, make-up can make the character seem more convincing. Some of the make-up used in films takes hours to apply because it has to look real when the actor's face is seen in close-up on the screen. Make-up artists do this job, and it can be very uncomfortable for the actor. Stage make-up has to produce its effect on the audience from a distance, so it is usually simpler and bolder than film make-up.

People have always tried to change the appearance of their faces as they acted out a story or a play. Long ago, ancient hunters wore the head or the skin of an animal to act out a story of catching their prey. The Iroquois Indians of North America wore "False Face" masks as they shook rattles and danced to drive away evil spirits.

False Face masks were worn by professional healers among the Iroquois Indians. They danced violently to drive away demons who were thought to plague the tribe. The faces of the masks are twisted and grimacing and they often have long horsehair wigs.

More than two thousand years ago, when Greek actors gave a play, they wore masks to show the character they were playing. Only men and boys could act in a Greek play. Women and girls were not allowed on the stage. The men and boys had to take all the parts, so they wore a mask to show if they were playing a boy or girl, a man or woman.

The masks also showed what the characters were feeling. There were smiling masks to show joy, frowning masks to show anger, and many other kinds of masks. We still use smiling and frowning masks to symbolize comedy and tragedy or acting in general. You sometimes see these masks printed on theater programs.

Masks were worn by Greek actors—there were no actresses. The masks represented the features of the character being played.

We still wear scary or funny masks on Halloween, but we do not now usually see them in the theater. However, in traditional Japanese drama, the performers still wear masks. There are several different types of Japanese drama. The most famous type is called No or Noh, which means "accomplishment." It is very noble in tone and stately in movement. The actors have to move like dancers and they are accompanied by drums and a flute. The stories used in the

Japanese Kabuki theater features music, dance, and spectacular costume. It originated in the late 16th century and is still extremely popular today.

No plays come from ancient tales about gods and warriors and noble courtiers. They are tragic in mood, but have little plot.

Another type of Japanese theater is called Kabuki. The name comes from the words *ka*, *bu*, and *ki*, meaning "singing," "dancing and "acting." There is more action and excitement in Kabuki plays than in No, although they are still very formal compared with Western drama. In both No and Kabuki plays, all the actors are men. In No the actors wear wooden masks when playing female parts and for some other roles. It takes a great deal of skill to perform successfully in these plays, and actors begin their training in childhood.

Puppets and Marionettes

In addition to No and Kabuki, there is a third type of Japanese traditional drama—the puppet theater. Puppets are found in many parts of the world, but it is mostly in Asia that they are considered a serious art form. India and Java are among the other places in Asia that are renowned for skill with puppets. In America and Europe, puppets are now used mainly in children's entertainment, although a few specialized theaters and groups put on full-scale puppet plays.

Japanese puppets are about two-thirds life-size and are controlled by teams of operators who are visible to the audience.

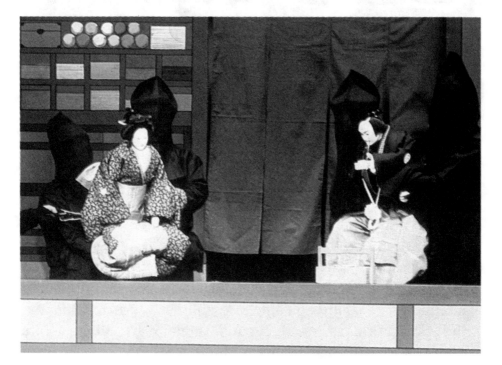

This scene from a Japanese puppet play shows the magnificent costumes that the puppets are dressed in. The puppeteers wear black clothes and hoods so that they do not distract from the puppets.

Each puppet needs two or three people to operate it, and it takes long training for them to achieve skillful coordination. The main movements of the puppets are controlled by a mechanism in the back, and the facial expressions can be changed by moving strings inside the body.

There are many other kinds of puppets. Marionettes are dolls controlled from above the stage by fine wires or strings. Rod-puppets, in contrast, are controlled from below the stage with thin rods. Shadow-puppets, or silhouettes, are flat shapes controlled with a rod fastened to the back. You can easily make them by cutting out shapes from cardboard and taping a straightened wire coat hanger to the back. For the stage, you need something like an old bed sheet or a white window shade tacked to a frame. If you shine a bright light from behind the silhouettes, the people on the other side of the screen—the audience— see the shapes as bold black patterns against a white background. You move the figures around to tell the story, using whatever action and dialogue you like. You can use a story that the audience already knows, or make up one of your own.

In the Islamic countries, shadow plays have been popular since the 13th-century, although today they are performed only at certain times of year. They are usually satires that poke fun at an assortment of stock characters. Only the outlines of the plots were scripted, and the puppetmasters made up comic dialogue as they went along.

Hand-puppets, or glove-puppets, are the simplest type. The ones that you buy have a head and hands attached to a loose costume open at the bottom. You put your hand inside the costume; your first finger goes inside the head, and your thumb and second finger each go in one of the puppet's hands. This means you can control one puppet with each of your hands and act out scenes between them. You can easily make simpler hand-puppets using an old sock for the body and odds and ends (such as buttons) for the eyes and other details.

Performing
a Play

It is exciting to watch a play, but it is even more exciting to give a play of your own. One of the best things about a play is that so many different people can be involved in so many different ways. You don't have to be one of the actors. You can help with making the scenery or just give a hand moving things into position on stage. Everyone can take part.

The first thing you have to decide is which play to perform. You can act out a play that someone else has already written or you can make up one of your own. If you like, you can act out a story from a favorite book.

Who else helps to create a play? If you give a play in school, a teacher usually helps you plan it and pick a player for each part. The teacher also helps the actors to speak their lines clearly and with good timing and makes sure that everyone is in the right place at the right time.

Your teacher is therefore like both the producer and the director in the professional theater. The producer is usually responsible for administration, such as financing the play and hiring the actors, and the director has the job of making the play an artistic success. Each director has his or her own way of understanding a play, but a good director always thinks of the playwright who wrote the play and tries to help the actors to act out the play in a way the playwright would want it performed.

If you decide to have a stage set for your play, you will need to have someone to design and then make it. This may be a job for several people, rather than just one. If you want costumes, someone will have to find them or make them. Professional theaters (and also some amateur dramatic societies) often have their own collections of stage clothes, but even very well-equipped theaters will never have in stock all the clothes they need for every play, so they will have to find them elsewhere or make them specially.

The room in a theater in which the actors' clothes are kept is called the wardrobe. The person in charge of it is called the wardrobe master or wardrobe mistress. He or she has to make sure that the clothes are well cared for and quickly repaired if they are ever damaged. Other people look after the stage props in the same way.

Plays are sometimes set in the theater. This is a scene from *The Dresser*, which deals with the relationship between an aging Shakespearean actor and the younger man who attends him in his dressing room.

Who else do you need to help you create your play? You will need stage hands to help move the scenery on and off stage, and if you have special lighting, you will need someone to make sure it is switched on and off at the right time. The lighting in theaters is

Musicals often have very spectacular sets. This is a set from Andrew Lloyd Webber's *Cats*, first performed in 1981. The use of computer controlled lighting effects and dramatic scenery are important elements in the presentation of an exciting show.

often very complex, with many different types of light, so an electrician takes care of it.

You will want people to know that you are giving a play, so perhaps someone could design a poster announcing when and where it will be performed. You could even make some programs, making sure that everyone who has helped with the play is mentioned in it.

The audience, too, has a part in making a successful play. The best type of audience is enthusiastic but well-behaved. People laugh at the jokes and clap in the right places, but keep quiet the rest of the time, so everyone can hear clearly what is being said on stage. This kind of audience encourages the actors to give their best and helps the occasion to come alive.

The Movies

A scene from *Jurrasic Park*, one of the most successful money-making movies of the 1990s. Dramatic special effects were used to create life-like prehistoric animals.

Hooray for Hollywood!

Marilyn Monroe (1926-62) was one of the most glamorous of all movie stars.

A few actors have had equally fine careers on stage and in films, but most of them specialize in one or the other. Some actors enjoy performing live on stage more than anything else. They love the sense of excitement and the feeling of contact with the audience. Other actors prefer making films. They like being able to do scenes several times until they get them just right. Some of them like the idea that millions of people can see their performances. Even if a play runs for months and months, only a few thousand people will see it in that time.

The first motion pictures made for entertainment appeared in the 1890s. They were very short and at first were shown as part of vaudeville shows. Then in 1902, a theater in Los Angeles began showing nothing but films. It was a great success, and theaters all

Charlie Chaplin (1899-1977) was the greatest star of the silent cinema. He first appeared in films in 1914 and was soon so successful that he directed all those in which he appeared. The character of a tramp that he created became famous all over the world.

over the country began doing the same thing. The first real movie theater, built specially to show films, opened in Pittsburgh in 1905. This, too, was very popular, and other movie theaters were soon built.

At first, moving pictures were such a novelty that people would come to see almost anything, but soon film makers began producing stories. They were silent stories, because there was as yet no way of adding sound to the film. This, however, had an advantage, because it meant that the same film could be shown in any country—there was no language barrier. Some of the earliest movie stars, for example the comedian Charlie Chaplin, did indeed become famous and popular all over the world.

Early films had to be shot entirely out of doors because the type of film used then was not very sensitive to light and would work properly only in bright sunshine. This is why Hollywood became the "capital" of the movie industry in America. The California sunshine was perfect for filming, and there was impressive scenery nearby, ranging from mountains to deserts, to make good settings for the stories.

In the early days of movies, the camera stood still and the actors simply played out their scenes in front of it. Film makers soon learned that by moving the camera they could make the pictures on the screen look much more varied and interesting. For example, close-up shots, in which the face of an actor filled almost the whole screen, could look very dramatic and show the actor's facial expression in detail.

The most important change in the history of the movies came in the late 1920s, when the first sound films were made. "Talkies" soon replaced silent films, and the movies became more popular than ever. The "golden age" of Hollywood movies was the 1930s and 1940s. Thousands of movie theaters and drive-ins were built all over the country, and millions of people went to the movies regularly at least once a week. In 1938, for example, the average number of tickets sold each week in the United States was 80 million. At this time, the population of the whole country was about 120 million.

To meet this huge public demand, Hollywood produced films at an amazing rate. In 1938, more than 500 films were made there. The studios had to work with great efficiency to be able to keep up this kind of production. Even a major film could be made with a speed that now seems hard to believe. For example, in 1933 the Metro-Goldwyn-Mayer (MGM) studio produced a film called *Queen Christina*, about a 17th-century queen of Sweden. It starred Greta Garbo, the most glamorous and highly-paid actress of the period, had a large cast, and was very lavish in its costumes and settings. Filming began on August 9, 1933, and ended on October 24, and the film was premiered in New York on December 26. Today, when people sometimes take months to shoot a short pop music

Both *Gone with the Wind* (above) and *The Wizard of Oz* (left) were made in 1939, when Hollywood was at a peak artisitically as well as commercially.

video or a television commercial, that kind of speed seems astonishing.

More routine movies were turned out by the studios in a matter of weeks rather than months. It is therefore not surprising that many of the films of this period were nothing special. There were many gangster movies and Westerns that did not differ much from dozens of others of the same type. However, the overall standard of skill was remarkably high, and some of the Hollywood films of the 1930s and 1940s rank among the finest ever made. They include the famous monster movie *King Kong* (1933); *Gone with the Wind* (1939), one of the most popular romantic stories of all time; and *The Wizard of Oz* (also 1939), a wonderful children's film that has also been giving pleasure to adults for more than half a century.

Gone with the Wind and *The Wizard of Oz* were two of the earliest movies to be made in color. By the 1950s, competition from television (which was only available in black and white until the early 1960s) meant that more and more films were made in color. For the same reason, the movies experimented with different types of very large screens. Huge, colorful "epic" movies were meant to make people think that the small black-and-white television screen was a very poor relation. Some of these epics were very successful; *Ben Hur* (1959) is an example. However, television became more and more popular, and fewer and fewer people went to the movies. By 1968, only 20 million tickets were sold on average every week in the United States—a quarter of what had been sold 30 years earlier.

In the 1970s and 1980s, the movies started fighting back against television in another way. Again there was a fashion for films that

were exciting as sheer spectacle and which had to be seen on a big screen to show to their best advantage. Instead of the historical epics of the 1950s and 1960s, however, the movies now turned to a different type of adventure film to try to pull in the crowds. They often had a science fiction setting, and relied on spectacular "special effects" to amaze and thrill the audience.

"Special effects" is a very broad term refer-

The science fiction movie *2001: A Space Odyssey* used many innovative special effects.

ring to ways of creating illusions on screen. The methods can vary from ingenious use of everyday items to extremely expensive computerized manipulation of the film. Special effects are used in films more than most people realize; sometimes they are done so cleverly that the audience has no reason to suspect that what they are seeing is not "the real thing."

In one film, for example, some indoor scenes were shot in London in a building overlooking the River Thames. The sunlight reflecting on the water outside the windows produced a pleasant glittering effect on the walls and ceiling of the room. Later some extra, unscheduled scenes had to be shot in the studio, which was reconstructed to look exactly like the room in London (this was cheaper than sending the film crew back to England). Everything looked perfect except for the light, which did not match the original scene. One of the special effects experts solved the problem with a brilliant (and very cheap!) idea. He filled a tray with water and put some pieces of broken glass in it. When a light was shone on it and reflected into the replica room, it created just the right effect!

Usually when we think of special effects, however, we have in mind spectacular illusions that show us something we could not possibly see in real life. These illusions are as old as the movies themselves, and some very famous films have relied heavily on them. *King Kong* is an example. The giant ape that we see on screen is in fact a little model, no bigger than a doll. To create the illusion that it was moving, it had to be filmed a single frame of film at a time. After each frame, the position of the model was adjusted very slightly, and eventually when the film was run at normal speed, it looked as if the ape was moving. This job took incredible patience, because the model had to be adjusted and filmed thousands of times. However, it was worth the effort, because the effects are still extremely impressive.

The first major film in which special effects, rather than actors, were really the stars was *2001: A Space Odyssey* (1968). This was directed by Stanley Kubrick, but the person who, more than anyone else, has created the modern movie "blockbuster" is Steven Spielberg. This American director, producer, and writer first made a big impact with his film *Jaws* (1975), a thriller about a giant man-

Steven Spielberg (above) has made several of the most commercially successful movies, including *Jaws* (right).

eating shark. It was hugely popular with the public, and he followed it with other films that continued to break records at the box-office. They included two about humans making contact with space aliens—*Close Encounters of the Third Kind* (1977) and *E.T.* (1982)—as well as a series about an adventurous archeologist called Indiana Jones. The most commercially successful of all his films is *Jurassic Park* (1993), about dinosaurs coming to life in the 20th-century. The special effects showing these huge creatures looking completely real are among the most breathtaking in the history of the cinema.

Spielberg has done a great deal to revive the movies in the United States. The industry also flourishes in several other countries (India produces a huge number of films, for example), but today more people watch movies on television or on video than in movie theaters. For the real film fan, however, nothing can beat the special magic of watching a movie on a big screen in a "picture palace."

Making a Movie

The person in overall charge of the film is usually the producer, who makes the financial arrangements to pay for all the other people working on it. This can involve trying to persuade wealthy backers to invest in the film; if the film eventually makes a lot of money, the backers get a share of the profits. It is often the producer who finds the main actors—the "stars"—for the film. Famous actors can earn enormous fees for appearing in films, but a producer knows that these fees will be justified if the stars' popularity helps to make the movie a success.

Other actors are sometimes hired by a casting director, who has to know which actors are available at the right time and will be suitable for particular roles. Most films also have "extras"—people who appear in the background but do not speak. These are often members of the public rather than professional actors, but they are still paid for their services. In a crowd scene, there may be dozens, or even hundreds, of extras.

The director of the film controls the way the actors interpret the script and the way that the camera shows them. The head camera operator (often known as the director of photography) will often advise the director on technical aspects, such as the best way to light a scene. Another important person is the art director (sometimes known as the production designer), who is in overall charge of costumes, settings, and accessories. This role is especially important in films such as musicals or historical epics, which usually have lots of colorful costumes.

Sometimes one person has more than one role in making a film. In 1948, the famous British actor Laurence Olivier made a film of Shakespeare's play *Hamlet*. Olivier not only produced and directed the film, but also played the part of Hamlet! More recently, the American Kevin Costner was co-director, producer, and star of the highly successful film *Dances with Wolves*. Such versatility is rare,

Kevin Costner starred as a US Cavalry officer in the western movie *Dances with Wolves*. The movie won seven Academy Awards ("Oscars") in 1990.

but several well-known actors have also become successful as either directors or producers. Jodie Foster, Clint Eastwood, and Robert Redford are examples of major Hollywood stars who have taken up directing and shown that they have great talent behind the camera as well as in front of it.

A great deal of work goes into a film both before and after the actual shooting. The people in charge have to plan the order in which they will do things so that they do not waste time and money. All the scenes that are set in the same place are filmed together, even though they may eventually appear at different points in the finished film.

For example, if the action of a film moves back and forth between London and Washington, the film crew does not keep flying across the Atlantic. It makes one trip to London, during which it does all the needed location shots. Many of the scenes that appear to be in London or Washington will in fact be shot in a studio somewhere else, but to look really convincing, some scenes have to be done on location.

The same principles apply if the film crew is merely moving from one room to another rather than one country to another. Cameras, lights, and other pieces of filming equipment are heavy and cumbersome to move, and they require masses of electrical cabling. Once they have been set up in position, it makes sense to keep

This photograph of a film set shows the cameraman and several other members of the crew setting up a shot.

them there until all the shots required in that precise location have been made.

At the beginning and end of each shot, a "clapboard" is held up to the camera. This is marked with the number of the scene and other details, so that afterwards each piece of film can be put in the correct order. The clapboard has a hinged arm on top; this makes a sharp noise when it is clapped down and provides a reference to make sure that the sound is properly synchronized with the picture.

After the shooting has been completed, a person called a film editor is in charge of putting all the separate shots together. This job can be as important as the director's, because the editor has to try to transform the film from a large number of individual components into a seamless work that seems to flow naturally. A quick change from an ordinary shot to a close-up, for example, can be very dramatic, but if it is not done skillfully it can look jerky. The editor also has to deal with dubbing music and other sounds onto the film, and sometimes with special optical effects.

Music is often very important in helping to create the moods of a film. Even in the days of silent movies, there was usually a pianist in the theater to provide a suitable accompaniment for what appeared on the screen, changing the type of music as the film moved from scene to scene. Some of the best composers of the 20th-century have written film music. The great Russian composer Sergei Prokofiev, for example, wrote the music for Sergei Eisenstein's famous film *Alexander Nevsky* (1938) and for several other movies. The American composer André Previn has composed scores for many Hollywood movies.

The famous futuristic opera
house at Sydney, Australia,
dominates the harbor waterfront

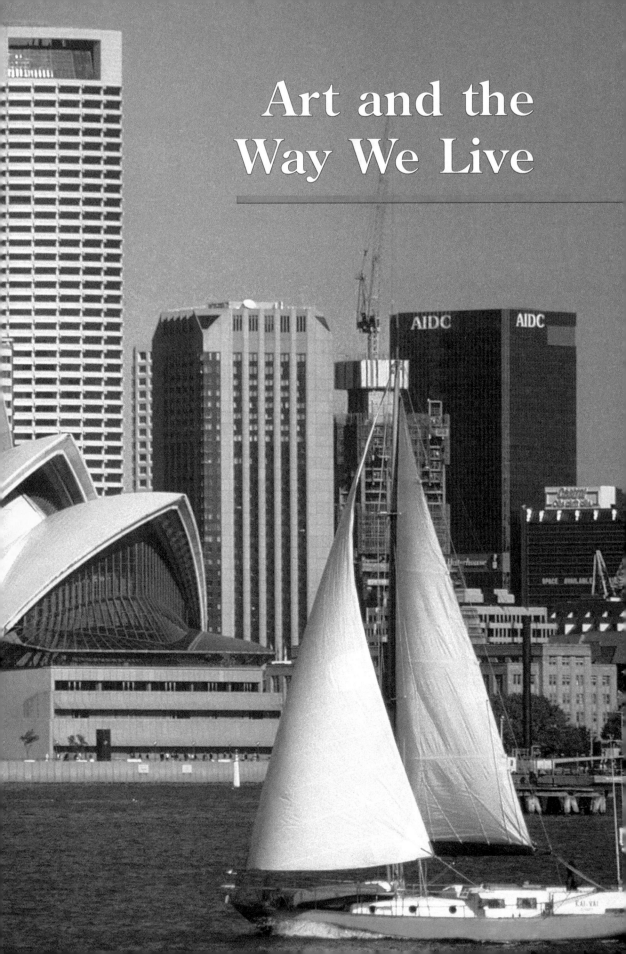

Art and the
Way We Live

The Clothes
We Wear

The clothes we wear are part of the way we live. An Eskimo (or Inuit) boy of the frozen north dresses differently from a boy who lives on the hot sands of the Sahara desert. A girl of today dresses differently from a girl who lived 100 years ago.

Like costumes in a play, the clothes we wear tell much about us. Often they tell where we live. They tell much about how we live and work and play. Clothes help us keep warm when it is cold. They help us feel cool when it is hot. They help us keep dry when it is raining. We wear different kinds of clothes when we go to school or to a party, when we swim or ride horseback.

Clothes help us in another way. Long ago when a cave man killed an animal, he wore its skin proudly, because it showed he was a mighty hunter. Today we still like to wear clothes that help us feel proud and happy. We like to wear clothes that make us look and feel attractive.

Artists help us do this by creating the styles of the clothes we wear. We call these artists fashion designers. Some fashion designers are men. Many others are women. Like a painter, a fashion designer works with colors and shapes. She works too, with materials of many kinds—silks and cottons, furs and wools, leathers and plastics, and many others.

A fashion designer creates a kind of picture and you are part of the picture. She creates the style of the jeans or dress, the shoes and sweater, and everything else you wear. A tall boy needs a different kind of style than a short boy. A thin girl needs a different kind of style than a chubby girl. The fashion designer creates different kinds of styles to help each of us look attractive.

The Rooms We Live In

The clothes people wear tell much about them. The way a room looks tells other things. Usually we plan the way our own room looks. Some people plan, or design, rooms for others. These people are called interior designers or interior decorators. Like other artists, they make a plan or design, and carry it out with shapes, colors, and materials of different kinds.

Let's pretend you are seeing your room for the first time. What do you see? Is it big and square or long and narrow? Is it light and airy? Where are the windows? Where are the lamps? Are they in the

This room has been furnished and decorated without much thought. Colors and patterns clash and the effect is jumbled.

right place to give you the best light when you read or study? What pictures are on the wall and where are they placed? What colors are the wallpaper, the rug, and the spread on your bed?

How does the room make you feel when you look at it? Does it give you a happy feeling? Interior decorators think of all these things when they design a room. They try to see the room as a whole so that everything in it fits together. They plan the colors and materials to use and where the furniture should be placed.

Interior decorators have to think carefully about how a room will be used. A kitchen and a living room and a bedroom need different things in them. They think, too, of the people who will use the rooms they design. Each person needs different things around him or her. A girl's room will be different from a boy's room. A baby's room will be different from a teenager's room.

What does your room tell other people about you? Do you have pictures of your favorite actors or singers on the walls? Do you like to build

model planes or collect souvenirs from places you have visited? Your room would tell that. If you were an interior designer, what changes would you make in your room? It is fun to plan and arrange a room the way you want it to look, and often it takes a little imagination.

Here the same room as shown on the previous page has been decorated and furnished with care, so that the colors and patterns are coordinated.

The Art of Handicraft

For thousands and thousands of years, people have been making things with their hands or with simple hand tools. Their art is called handicraft. Long before written history began, the people who lived in caves made stone axes and hatchets. At first, they did not care how these tools looked. They just wanted them to be useful.

Later, they began shaping tools that were graceful as well as strong. When they made a harpoon, they carved a reindeer or other animal on it. Then people who lived at a later time began weaving baskets and decorating them with patterns. They used the baskets to hold food and other things. They made pottery and decorated it with designs of lines, zigzags, or dots. That was the beginning of handicraft as an art. Ever since then, in countries all over the world, people have been carving, weaving, molding pottery, and shaping bronze and silver into shapes of their own design.

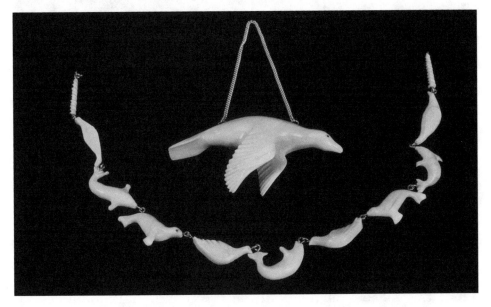

This jewelry carved from bone is a fine example of Eskimo (Inuit) handicraft.

Like painting, music, drama, handicrafts tell much about the artists who created them and when and where and how they lived. Before the invention of machinery, everything people used had to be made with the hands or with simple hand tools. Each person worked alone or with a few helpers. Each thing was made separately, and no two things ever came out exactly alike.

A woman sat at her loom and wove the cloth for the clothing her family wore. She wove the blankets and spreads for the bed and the rug for the floor. Often as she wove, she created her own designs.

In medieval times, a queen wove, too, and directed her ladies-in-waiting in weaving. The stone castle walls were cold, so coverings were often woven to hang on the walls and make the room warmer. These coverings, or tapestries, were decorated with patterns or with pictures woven into them.

Tapestries make a magnificent wall decoration at Hatfield House, one of the finest English stately homes built in the early 17th century.

The most famous "tapestry" in the world is not in fact a tapestry at all. It is called the Bayeux Tapestry, but it is embroidered with needles rather than woven on a loom. Really, we should call it the Bayeux Embroidery rather than the Bayeux Tapestry, but it has been called this for centuries, so it is too late to change now. It is a strip of linen, more than 200 feet (60 meters) long, embroidered with scenes depicting the story of the Norman invasion of England in 1066. This is the most famous date in English history. Duke William of Normandy ("William the Conqueror") defeated King Harold of England and became King of England himself. The tapestry was probably made for his half-brother, who was Bishop of Bayeux in France. It is amazing that it has survived in good condition for almost a thousand years. It was probably made by a team of English needlewomen.

This section of the famous Bayeux Tapestry shows Halley's comet appearing in the sky. The tapestry is over 200 feet (60 meters) long.

Until the invention of machinery, pottery, too, was made by one man or woman working alone or with helpers. Some potters shaped the clay by hand to make a pot, pitcher, or jar. Other potters shaped the clay on a potter's wheel. Often potters created shapes of their own design and decorated them with their own patterns. These designs and decorations help tell us when and where a potter lived. The ancient Greeks made many different kinds of pots in all shapes and sizes. Often they were decorated with paintings that show us scenes from everyday life. Some pots even depict potters and painters at work. Other Greek pots are decorated with pictures of gods and goddesses. Thousands of these pots survive and can be seen in museums all over the world. Many of them are fairly commonplace, but the finest ones are decorated with small masterpieces of painting. Almost all large-scale Greek painting has been destroyed, so vase paintings are very important to our understanding of Greek art. Pottery is often important in this way to

This scene from a Greek painted pot shows combat between two warriors. The figures are very elegantly drawn and are full of life.

people studying ancient societies. Although it breaks easily, it does not rot, so it can be buried in the ground for hundreds or even thousands of years and still survive in good condition. For some periods and peoples, pottery is the main source of knowledge we have of their culture, because little or nothing else has survived.

Handicraft may be a chair or a cup, a sword or an enameled locket. It may be a bedspread or a glass goblet. It may be a carved jewel box or a silver salt cellar or many other things we use. Once all the things people used were made by hand. Today most of the things we use are made by machinery. Thousands of articles are made from one design. We call this mass production. It is a quick and economical way to make things. Today we buy most of the things we need and use, but handicraft artists still weave and carve, mold pottery and shape metal to designs they create. It is exciting to create a design and make it yourself with your hands.

The Industrial Arts

Today we live in a world of machines and mass production. New arts have arisen because of this. These are called industrial arts. The handicraft artist creates an object by himself. The industrial artist, or designer, creates designs that are made by machinery through mass production.

Did you ever wonder how you would design a car? You can draw a picture of a car on paper. That is easy. But will the car be strong and swift and safe to drive? Will it be easy to drive and comfortable to ride in? What materials will you use to make it so? Will machines be able to make the car quickly and cheaply from the design?

Industrial designers must know the answers to all these questions. They know about materials and keep trying to find new ways of using them. Each material is different. Wood and steel and plastic look different and are strong in different ways. Glass and paper

This car is going through tests in a wind tunnel, which helps the designer to perfect an aerodynamic shape. The overall design of the car is perfected by correction and refinement.

and rubber take different shapes and are useful for different things. Industrial designers must also know about machinery, because their designs will be produced by machines. Their designs must make it easy for the machines to turn out thousands of cars or other objects swiftly and well. The industrial designers must know, too, what actions people make as they work and play. They must fit their designs to match the actions. Then the objects they help to create will be easy for people to use.

When mass production began, there were no industrial designers. The kinds of designs handicraft artists created were used. As industrial art grew, artists began to realize that machine-made objects needed a different kind of design.

Today many industrial designers are trying new ways to make designs that are right for machines. They are creating designs that are beautifully simple and strong and that machines can reproduce easily. They are helping create objects that people can use easily, too. The industrial arts tell much about the changing way we live.

Even the most commonplace items can be well designed and interesting to look at. This photograph shows plastic packing material that has been designed to be both durable and elegant.

Manufacturers of all kinds of goods now pay a great deal of attention to the appearance of the things they make. They realize that their products are often very similar in performance to the products of their competitors, so to try to make sure their own goods appeal to the buyer, they want them to look as attractive as possible. They think that if two radios, cars, or kettles do their jobs equally well and are the same price, you will choose to buy the one that looks best. Therefore, industrial designers can play a large part in our lives, although we do not usually consciously realize this. Industrial designers rarely become as famous as leading artists in other fields, but some of them achieve much bigger "audiences" for their work. The man who did more than anyone else to establish industrial design as a profession was Raymond Loewy. He was born in Paris, but he emigrated to the United States in 1919, and started his own design firm in New York City ten years later.

He did so many successful designs for so many different companies that at one time it was probably hard to go more than a day or two without using, or at least seeing, one of his products. His work included packaging for cigarettes and toothpaste, and household equipment including refrigerators, furniture, and lighting. He also designed Studebaker automobiles and was a consultant for the Greyhound Coach Corporation.

The famous industrial designer Raymond Loewy is shown with one of the railroad locomotives he designed.

Art and Architects

The cups and saucers, the tables and chairs in our houses are designed by handicraft artists or industrial designers. Did you ever think of your house as a design, too?

In the days of the pioneers, men went into the wilderness and cut down trees and built their own houses. They used the materials they found around them to build sturdy shelters against snow, wind, and rain. Usually they did not think of the way the house looked.

Today an artist called an architect designs a house. Architects too,, think of strength and safety. They use old and new ideas and materials to make the house light and airy, warm in winter, and cool in summer. Architects think of more than this. They know that people want more than shelter from their houses. People want beauty and grace around them. They want homes that reflect the way they live.

The architect thinks of a house as a design. The way the house looks inside is part of the design. The outside of the house is also part of the design. The architect knows, too, that a house does not stand alone. It is part of the countryside or of the city around it. Architects plan one kind of house for a hilltop and another kind for a seashore and still another kind of house for a city street. They think about climate, too. A house for a very hot climate and a house for a very cold climate will need different designs.

Architects ask many questions as they plan a house, but always they remember one important thing. A house is for people. Who will live in the house the architect is designing? Will it be an apartment building where many families live or will it be a house for just one family? How much money can the people spend to build the house? What kind of family will live in it? Will there be small children? Then the architect must plan space for them to play in and space for them to grow in. Families grow in size, too, and the architect must plan for this as he designs a house.

What do the people like to do? Do they like to read or play music or play games? An architect tries to fit his design to the people who

This picture of San Francisco shows an interesting contrast of building styles, with ornate Victorian houses in the foreground and skyscrapers on the skyline behind.

will live in the house. Architects design many other types of buildings, including hospitals and libraries, factories and office buildings.

Like a sculptor, an architect creates a form that has shapes and thickness. You can walk around a sculptured figure or a building. You can touch the roughness of stone or brick or the cool smoothness of marble. A sculptor molds or carves or shapes his figure. An architect creates a design that other people will build with stone, glass, brick, wood, steel and many other materials. Both are artists.

Different types of buildings are used in different ways. Architects use many shapes and materials in creating their designs, but always they try to fit the shapes and materials to the way the building will be used.

Like art, music, and drama, the buildings around us reflect the ways we live. Architects design buildings, but they do not build them themselves. Many people work together to do this. We rarely think of these people as artists, yet they help create the building. Each has a special kind of work to do. Without this work, there would be no home or school or church or skyscraper.

The Lloyd's building in London is a good example of "hi-tech" architecture. Its unusual design has most of the service shafts and piping on the exterior of the building as integral features. The building, which was designed by the British architect Richard Rogers, looks particularly dramatic at night when it is floodlit in blue light.

How many parts does a building have? You can see some parts, and cannot see others, but they help make the building strong and safe and ready for you to live, work, and play in.

You cannot see the foundation because it is under the building. The foundation must be strong, because it helps support the weight of the building and all the things and people in it. Construction workers erect the girders, beams, and columns; like the bones of a body, these help the building stand up straight and strong. Workers put up the outer walls and the roof of the building, then the inside walls and the ceilings.

Carpenters put in doors and window frames. Electricians install electric-outlet boxes and wiring. Plumbers put in pipes for gas, water, and sewage. Workers install equipment to give us heat. They also put in the air-conditioning units. Painters paint both the inside and outside of the building.

All these and many other kinds of workers help create the buildings we live and work in. They help create the libraries, museums, and hospitals. They help carry out the design of the architect. Another important worker who helps create the building is the contractor, who hires the people who work on the building and buys the materials they use. The architect, the contractor, and all the workers play their parts in creating the buildings we live in and use.

The Towns We Live In

Your town forms a kind of design, too. Houses, schools, churches, and other buildings make shapes against the sky. Trees and parks make shapes, too. Streets make straight or curved lines.

It is like a design for a stage setting, and the people in the town are the actors on the stage. Traffic hums on busy streets. Men and women work in homes and stores, offices and factories. Boys and girls work and play. Daily dramas are everywhere.

Many people plan and work together to make a town or city a safe, busy, and pleasant place to live. Usually we do not think of these people as artists, yet they create the design for the towns we live in. They can plan schools, libraries, and hospitals. They can plan parks and playgrounds, too. They can plan streets that are wide and smooth so traffic will flow swiftly and safely, and they can specify that trees be planted to shade the streets.

St. Louis, Missouri, was founded in 1764. This aerial photograph shows the grid layout typical of many American cities.

They can also plan convenient shopping centers and parking lots. They can pave the parking lots and decorate them with shrubbery, because they know that stores are busier when shopping facilities are made pleasant.

Cities usually grow gradually over a period of many years, but occasionally a new city is created out of nothing. The most famous modern example is Brasília, the capital of Brazil. It was planned in 1956 and officially became the capital of the country in 1960, replacing Rio de Janeiro. Brazil is a very large country, and the idea of moving the capital from the coast to virtually the center of the country was to encourage the economic development of the interior. The

The National Congress Building is one of the many fine examples of modern architecture in Brasília, Brazil.

place where Brasília was built was previously almost a wilderness, so the city's layout could be very spacious. The overall design of the city was by Lucio Costa, and many of its major buildings were designed by Oscar Niemeyer. Their work has been greatly admired, and many people regard Brasília as one of the most handsome cities in the world.

We do not know when people first started planning cities. Probably it was thousands of years ago. Ancient Athens, in Greece, was built on a high hill to make it easy to defend against enemies. Many other Greek cities also grew around a good defensive position. In medieval times, cities were built around a central market place. Walls were built around the city to keep it safe. All the people lived inside these walls. As the city grew, it became crowded. Some people began settling outside the walls. The city had outgrown its plan.

Later, people forgot a city had to have a plan. Cities just grew and grew. We still have cities like these. Buildings are crowded together. Traffic crowds the streets. There is little space to park a car.

Neighborhoods change as a city becomes crowded. A street of pleasant homes and gardens often turns into a street of dirty factories and dilapidated houses. Because there are not enough houses, poor people who live in these run-down neighborhoods are crowded together. When too many people live in one place, it becomes dirty

George Washington's house Mount Vernon, in Virginia, near Washington D.C. is a dignified example of 18th-century architecture.

The wedge-shaped Transamerica Building in San Francisco towers above the more traditional buildings around it, yet its unusual design makes the building an asset to the district rather than detracting from the character of the older buildings. The building is designed to withstand the effects of earthquakes, which occur quite often in the San Francisco area.

and unhealthy. Children who live there do not get enough clean air and sunshine to help them grow strong and healthy.

Like artists, city planners are trying to reflect the changing ways we live. While city planners try to change old towns and cities to make them safer and healthier places in which to live, they also try to keep some things unchanged. They know that each city, like each person, is different from every other city. Each city reflects the way the people in it live today.

Many cities also tell the story of how people in years past lived in them. Many cities help tell the history of a country. City planners try to keep old buildings that are part of our country's history.

In the Old North Church in Boston, the lanterns were hung that sent Paul Revere on his famous ride to warn the Minutemen of the American Revolution that the British were coming. Mount Vernon in Virginia was the home of the first U.S. president, George Washington. Abraham Lincoln's house in Springfield, Illinois, still stands. When we visit these historic places, we remember the great men who helped build our nation. The history of our country comes alive for us.

Some historic buildings are now used as museums to show how people lived long ago. Other ancient buildings are still used as they were when they were first built. Some churches are centuries old, but people still worship in them. The oldest churches in England date back to the seventh century, soon after St. Augustine introduced Christianity into the country. In America, one of the oldest churches is Bruton Parish Church in Williamsburg, Virginia, which has been in use since 1715.

Some homes, too, are hundreds of years old, but people still live in them. As you walk down a city street, often you can see an old building and a towering skyscraper side by side. Both help tell the story of a city and its people. Both are part of the picture of a city. Both reflect the way a city grows and changes as the way the people live changes.

A city and a town and a small village are different in many ways, but they are also alike in some ways. Each has homes and schools and churches. Each has places where people work and play. Each reflects the way the people in it live. Each helps tell the story of its country. Each is a part of the picture of its country.

The Way We Travel

To link the cities, towns, and villages in which we live, we build roads. The first great road builders were the Romans. They built roads linking their cities in Italy and in the other parts of Europe that they conquered. These roads were paved with stone. In open country they ran straight as an arrow for a great distance. One of the most famous Roman roads is called the Appian Way. It is named after a man called Appius, who began it in 312 BC. It ran from Rome to the southeast coast of Italy. Part of this great stone road still exists today.

The Incas, who ruled Peru before it was conquered by Spain in the 16th century, were great builders and civil engineers, too. They built more than 15,000 miles (24,000 kilometers) of roads to link places in their large empire. Some of these roads reached far up into the Andes Mountains, to an altitude of 17,000 feet (5,000 meters). For transport on land, they used llamas, loaded with packs of up to about 100 pounds (45 kilograms). To relay messages, they used teams of trained runners. These runners were stationed in little stone huts at regular intervals along the road, and they could travel more rapidly than a horseman in difficult steep countryside.

A road tells us much about the way the people who use it live. Before the invention of automobiles, most people traveled on foot or on horseback. Some drove wagons, carts, or stagecoaches drawn by horses. Today we drive cars swiftly from place to place. We build wide, strong highways for the cars to travel on.

Like the people who design our homes and the people who plan our cities, our highway builders are kinds of artists, too. They work with surveying tools and with gravel, concrete, and other kinds of materials. They try to make our highways strong and safe for cars

America's highways are among the great feats of 20th-century civil engineering. This aerial view of an interchange in California shows a dynamic abstract pattern, and illustrates the engineer's elegant design.

to travel on swiftly. They plan highways with few crossroads so cars can drive for long distances without a stop. This, too, helps make the highways safe.

Picture Acknowlegements

Graham Beehag: 2-3, 4-5, 10-11, 14, 15, 16, 17, 18, 20, 21, 23, 24, 25, 26, 29, 34, 35, 38, 39, 60, 61, 66 bottom, 67 bottom, 72 bottom, 73 bottom, 74-75, 79, 80, 84-85, 88, 170-171, 175, 183, 184. **Bridgeman Art Library, London:** 12-13 (Vincent Van Gogh *Ladies of Arles (Memories of the Garden at Essen)* Hermitage, St. Petersburg. 13 right (Vincent Van Gogh *Woman Stooping*) Rijksmuseum Vincent Van Gogh, Amsterdam. 19 top (Botticelli *Madonna of the Magnificat*) Galleria degli Uffizi, Florence. 19 bottom (Francesco Bassano *Building the Ark)* Wakefield Museums and Galleries. 22 (Jacopo Tinteretto *St. George and the Dragon*) National Gallery, London. 24 top (Samuel Cooper *Duchess of Orleans*) Victoria & Albert Museum, London. 27 (Giovanni Bellini *Madonna and Child with Saints*) San Zaccaria, Venice. 28 (Claude Monet *Woman with Parasol*) Musée d'Orsay, Paris / Giraudon. 30 (*Ikon of the Angel Michael*) Private Collection. 31 top (Giotto *The Lamentation of Christ*) Scrovegni (Arena) Chapel, Padua. 32 top (Edouard Manet *Monet in his Floating Studio*) Neue Pinakothek, Munich. 32 bottom (A.W. Hunt *A River Landscape*) Chris Beetles Ltd. London. 33 (Tommaso Masaccio *St. Peter* (detail). Brancacci Chapel, Santa Maria del Carmine, Florence. 37 (David Hockney *Mr and Mrs Clarke and Percy* (Ossie Clarke and Celia Birtwell). Tate Gallery, London. 40 top (John Constable *Elm trees in Old Hall Park, East Bergholt*) Victoria & Albert Museum, London. 40 bottom (Vincent Van Gogh *The Olive Trees*) Musée des Beaux-Arts, Tournai / Giraudon. 41 top (Edgar Degas *Café Concert at Les Ambassadeurs*) Musée des Beaux-Arts, Lyons. 41 bottom (Odilon Redon *The Buddha*) Musée d'Orsay, Paris. 42 (Kurt Schwitters *Mirror Collage*) ©DACS 1995. Private collection. 44 (Kurt Schwitters *Untitled* c.1923-25) ©DACS 1995. Scottish National Gallery of Modern Art, Edinburgh. 45 top (Piet Mondrian *Red, Yellow, and Blue Composition* 1930) Private collection, Zurich. 45 bottom (Hans Arp *Composition*) ©ADAGP, Paris, and DACS, London 1995, Christies, London. 49 top (Francis Bacon *Seated Man*) Tate Gallery, London/ The Estate of Francis Bacon. 49 bottom (Paul Klee *Flowers in Stone* 1939) Galerie Rosengart, Lucerne. 46 (Jackson Pollock *Yellow, Gray, and Black 1948*) ©ARS. NY and DACS, London 1995, Christies, London. 47 (Pablo Picasso *Woman Crying with a Handkerchief*) ©DACS 1995, Prado, Madrid. 54 bottom (G.S. Shepherd *The Royal Exchange and the Bank of England*) Guildhall Library, Corporation of London. 55 (*Hisaka in the Sayo Mountains*) British Library, London. 56 (Andy Warhol *Marilyn*) ©ARS, NY and DACS London 1995, Phillips, The International Fine Art Auctioneers. 57 (Pablo Picasso *Still Life Under a Lamp* 1962) ©DACS 1995, Christies, London. 58-59 (Henry Moore *Hill Arches 1963*) Yorkshire Sculpture Park, Bretton Hill. 65 (Alexander Calder *Oskkosch* 1965) ©ADAGP, Paris and DACS, London 1995, Mayor Gallery, London. 72 top (*Holy Women at the Sepulchre*) Victoria & Albert Museum, London. 73 top (Michelangelo Buonarotti *St. Matthew*) Galleria dell Accademia, Florence. 76 Victoria & Albert Museum, London. **James Sugar/Black Star/Colorific:** 191 **Eye Ubiquitos:** 138-39 (Paul Seheult), 180, 186 (Julia Waterlow) **Ford U.K.:** 179 **Hulton Deutsch Collection:** 108, 117 **Ronald Grant Archive:** 129, 158-59, 160, 161, 162-63, 164, 166 right, 168 **Eric Inglefield:** 63 main picture, 140 top. 151, 185, 188 **JNTO:** 152 **Mansell Collection:** 50-51, 54 top, 77 **Mirror Syndication International:** 169, 176 (BTA) **National Archives, Washington D.C.:** 78
Courtesy of Nikon: 83 **Linda Rich/P.A.L.:** 116 **Donald Cooper/Photostage:** 112, 138-39, 142, 143, 144-45, 146, 147, 156, 157 **Range/Bettmann:** 63 inset, 90-91 (UPI), 107 (UPI), 114 (UPI), 121 bottom (UPI), 123 (UPI), 126 (UPI), 127, 130 left (UPI), 181 (UPI) **Redferns:** 115 (David Redfern), 121 top (Derek Boulton Files), 122 top left (William Gottlieb), 122 top right (C. Stewart), 122 center right (David Redfern), 134 (Ebet Robert), 125 (UPI), 128 (David Redfern), 130 right (Ebet Robert) **Smithsonian Institution National Anthropological Archives:** 64 **Tate Gallery, London:** 66 top **John Walmsley:** 43, 48